A LIFE IN SUBUD

A Life In Subud

Raymond van Sommers

DAWN BOOKS
Australia

A LIFE IN SUBUD

Published by DAWN BOOKS
PO Box 531 Northbridge
NSW 1560 Australia

Reprinted 2004

National Library of Australia, Canberra ACT
Catalogue-in-Publication Information:

van Sommers, Raymond, 1928 -
A Life in Subud

ISBN 0 9751159 3 6

1. van Sommers, Raymond. 2. Spiritual Life. 3. Subud.

299.933

A contribution
to the history of Subud

The Meaning of Subud

From talks by Bapak Muhammad Subuh

SUBUD is an abbreviation of the words *Susila Budhi Dharma*. Subud is not a new religion, or a sect of any religion, nor is it a teaching. Subud is a symbol of the possibility for man to follow the right way of living.

Susila denotes those qualities which give rise to character, conduct and actions which are truly human, and in accordance with the will of God.

Budhi indicates that in all creatures, including man, there is divine power that works within him as well as outside him.

Dharma signifies sincerity, surrender and submission to the Will of Almighty God.

Susila Budhi Dharma means to follow the will of God with the help of the divine power that works both within us and without, by the way of surrendering oneself to the Will of Almighty God.

Contents

Acknowledgements

Bapak's received mission to establish Subud inspired my life since I first received the latihan. To the extent that this memoir contributes to his mission all thanks should go to Bapak.

To my sister Tess who was the perfect editor my love and gratitude for her professional help and familial patience. To Subud friends who read the archive version and encouraged me to see it as a book, Tony Bright-Paul and Hussein Rawlings, and to those that made valuable suggestions, especially David Week, Lilliana Gibbs and Blanche d'Alpuget, my warmest thanks. Finally to Harris Smart of *Subud Voice* magazine who suggested that the book would fill a place in Subud literature and undertook distribution, my ongoing appreciation.

The cover photograph is by Ulf Honold.

Raymond van Sommers

Prologue

Whereas my life started as an exploration of the world around me, it changed radically at twenty-six to a search for the purpose of life. As a result this memoir is as much about inner experiences as it is about outer events.

The ideas that triggered this change in 1954 were those of Ouspensky and Gurdjieff. Becoming a follower of their teaching with JG Bennett led me, three years later, to receiving the spiritual exercise of Subud and practising it for the rest of my life, including ten years in Indonesia with Pak Subuh (Bapak), the founder of the Subud movement.

The story is divided into two parts and a reference:

Part One contains an account of my Gurdjieff training, my childhood and my early working life, and the first twenty years after finding Subud and learning to follow the guidance of the *latihan* (spiritual exercise).

Part Two recalls the next twenty years, putting the latihan into practice in life—establishing and managing an enterprise and working with others in the role of a Subud helper.

The reference is part of a history of the Subud enterprise PT International Design Consultants in Indonesia during its first ten years, 1966-1976.

This memoir, as a record of my experiences, necessarily includes some observations about other people. If these offend in any way, I sincerely ask forgiveness.

Raymond van Sommers

A LIFE IN SUBUD

~

Part One

Chapter One

Coombe Springs

'Ah, you have come!' he said, fixing us intently with his light blue eyes. He seemed genuinely pleased. At two metres tall John Godolphin Bennett towered over us. I judged that he was about sixty, although his skin was still fresh and his brown hair showed few signs of grey. He had perhaps combed it back but now it stood out dishevelled as if by the wind. He had a broad forehead and strong clean-cut features, and a trimmed army-type moustache which reminded me that I had read he had been in British Intelligence in Turkey during World War I. He was wearing a baggy sports coat with leather elbow patches, and shabby corduroys. I heard a bell ring. 'We are about to assemble for lunch.' he said. 'Come and join us. Sit at the main table. Afterwards come to my study at three o'clock.' His voice was kind and encouraging. He strode away and up the stairs.

To get here my wife and I had made our way up the curved gravel driveway through trees and rhododendron bushes that screened the main house. We had made an appointment, and the tall wrought iron gates had stood open at the entrance. A glance at the long high red brick boundary wall, overhung with huge oak and chestnut trees, that ran down Coombe Lane to the left suggested privacy rather than security. The Edwardian gatehouse in brick and stone prepared us for a substantial main house. We were at Coombe Springs, at Kingston-on-Thames, near London, the premises of the Institute for the Comparative Study of History, Philosophy and the Sciences Limited—the name for the esoteric Gurdjieff school for the study of man's higher potential run by Mr JG Bennett.

Mr Bennett had first met George Ivanovitch Gurdjieff, from whom the teaching derived, in Constantinople in 1920. In London in 1921 he became a student of PD Ouspensky, a Russian pupil of Gurdjieff, and spent time with Gurdjieff in France in 1923. After working with Ouspensky he started his own study group in 1930 in London. His profession as a physicist led him, in 1934, to be appointed director of the newly formed British Coal Utilization Research Association (BCURA). During World War II German bombing drove BCURA out of London at a time when Mr Bennett was looking for a place for his study group. He arranged for Coombe Springs to be leased by BCURA for its laboratories and for the grounds to be used by the study group. When the war ended BCURA moved out and Mr Bennett and his pupils purchased Coombe Springs as a permanent centre for his school.

At the top of the driveway we had barely left the sound of our footsteps on the gravel and reached the entrance porch of the two-storey mansion when Mr Bennett had appeared in the hall.

Now people began coming into the porch from the garden, men and women in casual clothes, some with gardening boots. They moved deliberately and quietly towards the dining room. A short and plump middle-aged woman introduced herself to us as Kate, and asked us to go with her to the dining room. She showed us to seats at the end of the large main table, some four metres long, made of solid oak, amber-grey with use, and worn to reveal the grain.

The rest of the dining room was set up with bare, scrubbed timber trestle tables, laid with simple cutlery. There were two large glass bowls of salad and one of fruit on each, and wholemeal bread on a table near the entrance door. There were chairs for about forty people.

I was alert with excitement. I was, I felt certain, in the sanctum of the world's most secret school and among those who had discovered the purpose of our life on earth and how to wake up in a world that was asleep. It was the equivalent no less than being sighted in a land of the blind. It was 1 May 1955.

John G. Bennett, Director, Institute for the Comparative Study of History, Philosophy and the Sciences, Coombe Springs, UK.

Coombe Springs main house entrance (East side) 1955

Coombe Springs dining room 1955

The room quickly filled. Chairs scraped on the wooden floor. People were talking, but the room became quieter as Mr B (as Mr Bennett was called) entered. He took his seat in the centre of the main table with his back to the huge bay window that overlooked a rose garden. Even seated he was an imposing figure, radiating energy. I had already decided that he was in a continuous state of conscious self-awareness—a goal of the Gurdjieff teaching. He introduced us to the others at the table as coming from Australia and gave our first names, Jan and Ann, but not theirs. He spoke very distinctly, always looking straight at the person he addressed. There was one other guest from overseas, an older man who, it seemed, had known Ouspensky. This man sat on Mr B's right.

Several students, apparently rostered for the job, served us each with a plate of kedgeree. It smelt of smoked fish and hard-boiled eggs. Everyone fell silent for a full two minutes. Mr B moved first and began eating with the same larger-than-life energy that I had already noticed in all his movements. He talked with evident interest to the visitor on his right.

My kedgeree tasted good. I chewed every mouthful deliberately, trying to maintain awareness in the way that I had already learned from reading Ouspensky. By now there was a hum of conversation around the room. Just as I reached for a piece of fruit, Mr B shouted 'Stop!' I froze—simply out of shock—my hand resting on an apple. I saw everyone else had become like a waxworks figure. I held my breath. A minute later we were released. I realised it was some kind of exercise in self-observation.

'What did you see?' asked Mr B, addressing the question at large. There was an air of command about him, but charisma as well.

An attractive young women with a Dutch accent and a red and white Lapland sweater started to speak. 'At that moment', she said, 'I was thinking: "I am now *remembering myself*". But when the *Stop!* came I was startled. I saw that "I" wasn't *awake*. It was just my thoughts.'

'Ah, yes!' said Mr B. 'That is how it is. Often we are nothing but our thoughts.'

'Anyone else?' he went on. His tone suggested that, whatever our experience, it was important.

'I was day-dreaming about my work in the garden planting out pansies', ventured the woman I had seen in the driveway. Mr B said nothing.

Several others related their experience and then the room fell silent.

'All right then,' Mr B said, finally relieving the tension. 'What about this morning's exercise, how did you get on with that? Could you *remember yourself* at the given times?'

'After you called "Stop!" in the garden,' a young man began, 'I found that I could return to the state that I felt in the morning *preparation*.'

'That's how it should be.' said Mr B. 'Something was collected in the morning. It was like money in the bank. But what about at the predetermined times? That was the exercise. Did you manage to remember on each hour? '

'Something in me remembered,' said a bearded man at our table, 'but it was weak. I just thought, "It is the time," and immediately lost it. However, when the bell rang for lunch and I started to walk towards the house I suddenly had a clear experience of the morning *preparation*. It was after I had given up trying.'

'There you are,' said Mr B, 'you realise that the experience didn't come from nowhere. Your earlier efforts created the finer energy and, when you relaxed to come to lunch, it returned. We have to learn from experience. Little by little we gradually come to see what it is that gives results.'

The lunch and discussion had run for about an hour, when Mr B got up and brought the proceedings to a close. 'Good!' he said . 'This afternoon there will be *movements* here in this room at four thirty. *B Group* first.' He left the room swiftly, as if something else awaited him.

I felt stimulated, alert and alive. I was from my reading already familiar with many of the terms Mr B had used. *Movements*, sometimes known as temple dances, were exercises to music which were only possible to perfect in a state of higher consciousness.

Ann and I had an hour before our meeting with Mr B. We left the dining room through an adjoining conservatory and went into the rose garden. The house appeared to have about thirty rooms. Two wings towered over terraced lawns leading down into three hectares of gardens. Beyond the rose beds a path led into a glade of ancient trees, with patches of daffodils. Here, in a clearing, was the spring house that gave Coombe Springs its name, built by Cardinal Wolsey in the sixteenth century to supply water to Hampton Court. We went down a flight of steps to where water was spouting from a pipe in the wall into a stone tank. The splashing echoed in the high vaulted ceiling. Although everything was wet it was fresh and wholesome. Leaving the spring house we followed a small landscaped stream through some fruit trees and a substantial vegetable garden where people were working in silence. They ignored us as we passed. Further up the slope we found a long, single-storey pre-fab building with a wall of continuous windows, apparently used for accommodation. Later I heard that this was called *The Fishbowl* because people felt exposed by the windows. (It had been the BCURA research laboratory during World War II.) Beyond this was a newer two-storey brick building also for accommodation, with a Swedish sauna downstairs.

Now it was time for our appointment. We found Mr B in his study. He was sitting behind a large desk spread with papers and books, neither over-tidy nor disordered. The room was spacious, perhaps five metres by ten, with the same bay windows as the dining room below but commanding a view through the tree tops to the properties across Coombe Lane. It was carpeted with Persian rugs and uncluttered. There was a secretary's desk at the far end and shelves of books on the walls. He motioned us to sit in armchairs and joined us.

Again I noticed the intensity of his gaze.

'Tell me now,' he said, 'How did you hear about *The Work?*' (This was the term the Gurdjieff people used for their teaching.)

Stream from the springs in the garden at Coombe Springs

Weekend work in the orchard, Coombe Springs

Lawn under the great oak, Coombe Springs

The XVIth Century Spring House, Coombe Springs

As it had been I, not Ann, who had come across the Gurdjieff teaching, the brief history was mine:

'In March 1954 I sailed on a P&O liner back to Australia after a stay of four years in England and in West Africa. I was single and my main object in life had been to travel, enjoy myself and earn a living at my calling of engineer. I had never reflected seriously on the meaning or purpose of life. On the boat I fell into conversation with the ship's engineer. He lent me Ouspensky's book *In Search of the Miraculous,* which included an account of the ideas of the mysterious Caucasian teacher Gurdjieff.

'As I read it, suddenly it dawned on me—*I am.* Ouspensky's ideas not only momentarily *awakened* me but also posed the fundamental question of the very purpose of my existence and of human existence in general.

'At twenty-five I had been unexpectly roused from simply being awake in the normal sense to glimpsing a state of self-consciousness where *I am* had a new meaning and validity. The experience was as if I had been asleep to my own existence until then. This *waking up* was just as clearly defined from the normal waking state as was waking in the morning from ordinary sleep. Until that moment I had never experienced myself self-consciously, that is, with any sense of objectivity. Ouspensky was right; our normal waking state was a sleeping state. I was a sleepwalker and didn't know it.

'Gurdjieff called the returning to this self-conscious state *remembering oneself* or self-awareness. Each time it happened it rudely confirmed that the rest of the time I was still asleep. It was shocking to know that I was unconscious of myself and that life was just happening to me without my participation. I had to find a way out of this situation. *Remembering myself* became what Ouspensky called a burning question.*

* CG Jung calls this conversion *enantiodromia*—a psychological flip from one extreme to its opposite which can happen when a person is totally identified with their outer life image to the exclusion of any awareness of their inner life (soul).

'As soon as I was home in Melbourne I read all the Ouspensky books I could find. In his six lectures published as *The Psychology of Man's Possible Evolution*, he proposed that nature has brought humanity to a certain point and from there on it is up to people themselves to develop certain inner qualities by their own efforts to become different beings. Help is needed from those have already started and attained a certain degree of development—hence *schools* (of esoteric knowledge). A Gurdjieff school, he said, consists of people dedicated to *waking up* and developing *self-consciousness, unity, permanent 'I' and will.* Only with these capacities could a person 'pay the debt of his existence' and contribute anything of significance to the welfare and destiny of humanity. I began to look for a Gurdjieff teacher and, through library references, came to know about Coombe Springs.'

'And how about you, Ann?' Mr B said kindly. Ann looked at me and then back to Mr B. 'Well, Jan told me about it, and it seemed right. We are just married, so we do everything together.'

'We have just formed a new study group—*Y Group*,' said Mr B. 'They are mostly young people like yourselves and you can join them. It meets once a week on Saturday afternoons and then of course you can come on Sundays for practical work with others. In the group you will do awareness and self-remembering exercises. Come early next Sunday and take part in the morning *preparation:* relaxation and sensing the body. About fees, speak to Kate. If you have a problem, pay what you can afford. Where will you live? Have you got a job yet?'

'We are living with my aunt in Sutton, and she will introduce me to Mr WF Rees, chairman of the Federation of Civil Engineering Contractors, a family friend. Perhaps he can help,' I said.

'You can watch the *movements* at 4.30,' Mr B said and got up. We thanked him and left the room.

Kate was in the office and recorded our contact address and telephone number and next of kin. She gave me a list of the members of Y Group. I was surprised to find that there were thirty one, plus three leaders. Ten lived at Coombe Springs.

The *movements* were in the dining room. We sat with several other pupils cross-legged against the wall and watched. The music sounded Middle Eastern. Some had been written by Gurdjieff, some by the Russian conductor Thomas de Hartmann, some were sacred dances collected from the Sufis. Most had a strong rhythm which I felt impelling my body to move. Only a mazurka was lyrical. The pianist was a tall, slim, elegant man, a professional concert performer from Australia. He played faultlessly, with passionate expression. The pupils, men and women in about equal numbers, in light clothing and soft leather heelless pumps, stood evenly spaced in three rows. Most seemed to be under thirty. In some *movements* the pupils followed a sequence of steps and arm positions out of phase with each other, which created a complicated pattern of ripples down the rows. In one they spun like dervishes.

That night I couldn't sleep. All that week I felt fired up by the images of my one long day at Coombe Springs.

In my twenty-seventh year, I believed I was about to discover, for the first time, who *I* was. What I had been until then was a plain enough story—and one that I was later to look back upon as, in a sense, two dimensional only.

~

Mr Bennett directing *movements* at Coombe Springs 1955

Gurdjieff students watching *movements* 1955

Donald Neil accompanying Gurdjieff *movements*, Coombe Springs

London presentation of Gurdjieff *movements*

Chapter Two

Childhood & Youth

I was born at *The Pines* hospital, Ringwood, on the eastern outskirts of Melbourne, Australia, on 21 November 1928 and given the name John van Sommers. My mother was twenty- four and my father, an artist and writer, was twenty-seven years her senior. Her memoirs suggest that she was idealistic and inexperienced in the ways of the world at the time of meeting my father.

My father had already been married before. He was a veteran of World War I, where he had served in Egypt and France. After the terrible experiences of the war in France he was discharged in February 1918 with a chronic chest illness—perhaps from being gassed in the trenches, or from trench fever—which later developed into pulmonary TB. He had a small Army pension.

As my sister Tess, who was nine when I was born, recalls, 'There is much speculation about our ancestors—an elopement with the Earl of Douglas's sister and a line of van Somer Court painters from the time of Charles II. Father told me his grandmother dressed him in the Douglas tartan and had a velvet jacket made for him with silver buttons that carried the Douglas crest. ... My father's father was an artist and teacher of drawing, and was a pupil and good friend of Fredrick McCubbin.'

John Charles Douglas Sommers or Jack Sommers, as my father signed his paintings, had as a young man studied at the National Gallery in Melbourne under its director Bernard Hall with such celebrated artists as George Bell, Max Meldrum and Chas Wheeler.

He knew the Lindsays well, having shared a studio with Norman Lindsay in Sydney. His work included Australian landscapes and regular illustrations for *The Lone Hand* magazine. After the war he painted portraits and worked as a part-time journalist contributing stories, verse and illustrations to *The Bulletin*.

Initially my parents set about buying and refurbishing a goldminer's cottage in Warrandyte. In spite of their meagre income from his painting and writing, my mother records that their early days were at times idyllic—a bush setting, riding horses, and occasional visits from other artists and writers of the period. My mother was riding every day until a month before I was born.

I was very close to my mother. She was the hub of the family, caring and responsible. Although she came from strict religious English parents of the Victorian period (they gave her the Christian name Grace) she was nevertheless an optimistic, practical and outgoing woman, charitable in her attitude to other people. This showed itself in her belief in, and support for, my father as an artist, and later in her success in helping refugees during the war and founding one of Melbourne's first women's community clubs.

By the time my brother Peter was born in 1930, life for my parents had become extremely difficult. The Great Depression meant that, where my father had had continuous private commissions as a portrait painter—and had just completed painting the heraldic scenes on the ceiling of the Regent Theatre in Melbourne—now he could not even sell his paintings. His health also deteriorated and for the last four years of his life we travelled in a horse-drawn wagon through inland Victoria and New South Wales seeking a warmer and drier climate.

My mother wrote about this period as an increasingly desperate time—a young inexperienced woman with the responsibility for a sick man, sometimes violent with the frustration and pain of his illness, a young girl not yet in her teens, and two small boys, one a baby, moving from place to place on outback roads, far from supplies for themselves and the two horses.

To what extent these first six years of my life moulded my character I can only guess. I was restless from an early age, exploring new places and new interests. I took on some aspects of my father's bohemian disregard for authority and convention, and his urge to please himself. I have his self-reliance and confidence. I do not have my father's explosions of temper, probably because these were not in the family line, but rather a result of his traumatic experiences in World War I. However, perhaps his outbursts have caused me to be extremely adverse to rough behaviour by others.

After my father died my mother returned home and Tess went to a boarding school. A year or so later my mother met and married Eric Thake, an artist her own age. He was a mild-natured man with regular work as an illustrator. Peter went to live with our grandparents (on my mother's side) and I stayed with my mother and stepfather. From that time on I enjoyed a happy family life, first living in Black Rock, a seaside suburb of Melbourne, and later in Ormond where Joan, my first younger sister, was born.

When my grandmother died in 1938 the family came together in my grandparent's house in East Kew. My grandfather was a cabinet-maker and a kindly man. His workshop was an Aladdin's cave where he made us all the toys of our childhood. These were still frugal times for everyone in Australia but we had enough. Peter and I went to the local State School for the remainder of 1938 and 1939, walking the two kilometres to school, idling on the way home on the swings and climbing-bars of the public playgrounds. In short, we had a normal childhood in a safe middleclass environment.

I remember little about these years of schooling, except for two social-studies projects. One was on the geography and people of the Dutch East Indies (later Indonesia). Its artistic layout shows that my stepfather helped me no small amount. I was fascinated by the exotic pictures in a way that nothing else in my early schooling touched me. I have never believed that the future is determined, but I must admit that it strikes me now as strange that I should have had this strong attraction to Indonesia, which was later to be so important in my life.

When Jennifer, my youngest sister, was born we moved to a larger house. The years that followed were stable and happy. I loved my family and occupied myself with various hobbies, particularly collecting butterflies. The house was on a typical Australian suburban quarter acre with a large back garden. We had fruit trees, grew vegetables and kept chickens. There was a swing and a sand-pit for my baby sisters. It was the days of radio and we would listen together as a family to the weekly nature programs.

My stepfather left parenting largely to my mother. He was absorbed in his art, spending most of his home life painting and engraving in his studio. The house was decorated by him with furniture that he designed and it was hung with his drawings, paintings and lino-cuts, beautifully mounted and framed. By exposure to his artwork we were all influenced by his artistic judgement and appreciation. As a well-known fine-artist he was soon appointed an official war artist in the Australian Air Force. This took him away to the Pacific Islands during the Japanese advance and retreat, only occasionally returning for leave until the war ended in 1945. Many of his paintings are held at the Canberra War Memorial and in State art galleries.

My mother pressed me to get a technical education. I believe this was in part a reaction to her bad experience with my father during the Depression. I went to Swinburne Technical College for my secondary and tertiary studies from 1940 to 1947, first studying practical trade and craft subjects—carpentry, metalwork, blacksmithing, clay modelling, etc—and then going on to take a diploma in civil engineering.

I enjoyed the outdoor activities of a teenager growing up in those times in Melbourne. From 1942 to 1948 my close friends came from the local Scout troop. We had weekly meetings and Saturday excursions—trekking, mapping, and nature study, finishing with a cookout. Once a year we went on a longer camp in the mountains. We also spent our spare time together, cycling and swimming in the local river. Movies were a rare treat.

Two incidents remain in my memory from those times which seem to have foreshadowed my disposition to religious experience and psychology. The first was at the dentist when I was thirteen. I was given nitrous oxide (laughing gas) as an anaesthetic to have two large teeth removed. This is as I now remember it:

I sat in the chair and, as the dentist tilted it back, another man in a white coat wheeled the gas equipment up to my face. Suddenly I felt very nervous. As I looked around for the nurse to give me reassurance, the man with the gas put a mask on my face.

'Take deep breaths,' he said.

I smelt the gas as I breathed. It was warm and slightly sweet and then, all at once ...

All was light, and everything was there and known. Then I was in darkness—nothingness, hopelessness and utter despair. Then I was in the light, then the darkness, then the light... Within a disk of black and white, spiralling to an infinite centre, I moved alternatively from light to darkness inwards, everything ... nothing ... everything ... nothing, forever.

I woke up struggling and felt someone let go my arm. The nurse and dentist were standing back a little. Very shaken, I saw around me fragments of broken glass and blood. There was consternation on the dentist's face. 'You gave us a bad time,' I heard him say. I staggered out, still more 'there' than here. I had been to a fearful place, a prison of the mind where I was trapped for eternity.*

* Years later I read *The Varieties of Religious Experience* by William James where he writes: Nitrous oxide when sufficiently diluted with air, stimulates the mystical consciousness in an extraordinary degree. Depth upon depth of truth seems revealed to the inhaler. This truth fades out, however, or escapes, at the moment of coming to; and if any words remain over in which it seems to cloth itself, they prove to be the veriest nonsense. Nevertheless, the sense of a profound meaning having been there persists.

Of his personal observations on nitrous oxide intoxication, he goes on: One conclusion was forced upon my mind at the time (of my experiences) and my impression of its truth has ever since remained unshaken. It is that the normal waking consciousness, rational consciousness as we call it, is but one special type of consciousness, whilst all about it, parted from it by the filmiest of screens, there lie potential forms of consciousness entirely different.

The back garden of our house in East Kew, Melbourne 1940-1950

My parents, grandfather and sisters seeing me off to England by ship in 1950

The second experience was a religious conversion when I was about fourteen. Although my grandfather was a committed Christian, teaching at the Sunday school and spending much time reading religious books and studying the Bible, his dedication had little effect on me. Strangely, it was when a boy at school showed me texts from the New Testament that I was overwhelmed with religious fervour. I was filled with a kind of elation and endlessly read the verses highlighted in my copy of the four gospels. I went into churches and prayed with charismatic intensity. This state ran for some months before it subsided.

I finished my fulltime study at Swinburne at the end of 1946 and, following a friend from my class, took a job with the engineering section of the Victorian Railways. The work was surveying and drafting for railway trackwork. I had a capacity for neatness and developed some skill in fine technical drawing—probably from my genes. Gradually I spent more time outdoors surveying track alignments and found going to new places exciting as I travelled around the country areas of Victoria. Somewhere about this time I began to be called Jan as a contraction of John van.

It was in 1948 during an assignment in Gippsland that I met a Dutch engineer who changed the direction of my life. He was an older man who had just returned from working in Indonesia. Surrounded by his souvenirs—paintings, carvings, and so on—and the trappings of his lifestyle including a large short wave radio, he puffed on cigars and talked with great enthusiasm about the huge projects that he had been responsible for in Indonesia and before that in South America. He advised me to study overseas and get international qualifications so I could work anywhere in the world.

I was very impressed, and once again there was this numinosity about Indonesia. I resigned from the Victorian Railways and took a job with an oil exploration team in Papua New Guinea, with the idea of saving enough money to study in England.

~

Chapter Three

Study, Work & Travel

At nineteen working in Papua New Guinea was a tremendous adventure and I revelled in it. Here I was in a remote and primitive land, virtually unexplored and unaffected by the outside world. In 1948 there were just twentyfive miles of road in the whole territory, and that was near the capital, Port Moresby. The only areas of development were the copra plantations along the coast, reached by boat. Elsewhere the island was covered with almost impenetrable jungle. It had extremely difficult terrain, from the inaccessible swamps of the large river deltas to the rugged foothills and mountain escarpments. It had a heavy rainfall, in some places amongst the highest in the world, which created enormous rivers winding through the jungle from the interior. Its people lived separately in hundreds of isolated tribes, speaking different languages and often hostile to one another.

Papua which comprised the south-east quarter of the island of New Guinea was administered by Australia through a Governor. It was policed by patrol officers who travelled by boat and on foot using local people as guides. The language of communication was *motu*, an adaptation of the Port Moresby dialect.

Evidence of oil had been noticed three or four decades earlier, but it was only after World War II that an oil company, Australasian Petroleum Company (APC), intensified the search with modern equipment. Drilling had started at Hororo in the south gulf country.

I joined APC's first geophysical survey of the upper reaches of the Purari River. The project was to map the underground geological strata by seismic refraction to try to locate potential reservoirs of oil.

Geophones were used to record the vibrations from dynamite explosions. I joined as a surveyor under Mr S.E. Evans, a Welshman who had been working in Persia. It was our job to fix the position of the geophone stations and explosion points, using aerial photographs, astronomical fixes and ground tacheometry.

The surveying turned out to be a minor aspect of the work. The logistics of getting to the area, supplying ourselves, and managing the labour force were the major tasks. Learning the language was another, it took several months. We took with us hired labour and supplies from Port Moresby. The people were recruited from several different tribes, including the famous 'Fuzzy Wuzzy' heroes of the Kokoda Trail. Some were tall well-built men from the coastal islands, some were shorter, from the river deltas. When our team of ten Europeans, including a doctor, was complete we were joined by two hundred of these Papuan workers.

To get to the inland site I travelled aboard a fifty-tonne steamer (a K Boat) along the coast and then up the Purari River. Standing on the plunging bow I delighted in the experience of the shallow draft vessel riding the swell of the aqua-coloured water of the Gulf. For the next thirty hours I was seasick until we bounced over the sand-bar into the quieter water of the river. Once we left the villages of the delta, the area was almost unpopulated.

We built our base camp about one hundred kilometres inland. Even so far upstream this large river was two hundred metres wide and could flood fifteen metres overnight. We chose high ground and cleared the dense jungle back from the river bank. The Papuans were experts at building with forest materials. They built us small thatched bungalows and storehouses and long shelters for themselves. They were issued with a cloth sarong and a machete and provided each week with a ration of food—rice and tinned beef—also tobacco twist, matches and simple trade goods. The rest of their payment was kept until the end of their contract. Medical attention was provided by the company.

For our work we were each allocated a 'line' of ten or twelve men as bearers and as workers to cut our way through the jungle. These were to be my only company at times for weeks as I surveyed and set up the position of the geophone stations. In those days the white person automatically assumed a role as headman over his labourers. This superiority was expected and depended on establishing mutual respect. We all created a close relationship with our line and were reluctant to let them work with anyone else. Many of the men were working for the first time away from their village. Only my cook had had any previous experience and that was in the civilisation of Port Moresby. As we progressed inland we moved into territory where white man had never been before. Occasionally the workers would get very nervous, saying that there were Kukukus, feared nomadic hunters, in the area. No one liked to be alone or at the end of a line for fear of being silently attacked by a poison arrow. We never saw anyone. Although I was the youngest member of the team, my bravado and perhaps my shotgun—which I carried to shoot wild pig and pigeons for fresh meat—strengthened their confidence.

The jungle was full of life, much of it unfriendly. Not only was the vegetation so thick that it closed out the light and entangled anyone that tried to pass with hooked vines, but it also crawled with biting insects. There were stinging flies and ferocious red ants and all kinds of spiders. As we cut our way through the dense foliage, we disturbed snakes (some poisonous, like the death adders) and pythons of various colours and sizes, some big enough to eat a cassowary (a type of emu) whole. For good measure there were leeches. On the river banks and up the creeks there were swarms of sandflies and mosquitoes. Scratches and leech wounds had to be carefully treated to avoid festering in the steaming humidity. We took prophylactic pills against malaria and depended on our clothing and insect repellent to avoid dengue and blackwater fever carried by another type of mosquito. In spite of all these hazards, it was a great adventure and I soon became adjusted.

Surveying in Papua New Guinea

On the Purari River 1948

Bearers with new dugout canoe on the Purari River

Bearers at Mena Bend base camp, Papua 1949

Village on the delta of the Purari River

Where possible we would use a creek as a route to a new site or travel by dugout canoe, either with paddles or for long journeys with an outboard motor. We carried adzes and the bearers could build these canoes in a few hours. Selecting a perfect jungle tree of a particular wood, they would fell it and cut out the inside to leave a thin strong shell, which they then launched on rollers into the river. Paddles were cut and carved with the same speed and dexterity. It is hard to describe the exhilaration of standing in a dugout canoe as it speeds down a jungle river with a dozen powerful natives singing and beating a rhythm with their long paddles.

There were many crocodiles in the big rivers and everyone took great care near the water. Some were huge, several metres long, and could run faster than a man on land. They were silent in the water and reportedly often took a villager off the bank.

I worked in three areas. The first was up the Purari River in rugged broken country with dense jungle. The second was further inland and higher up on the Mena River, and lastly I was in the swamps of the Purari delta. To get to the Mena we had to trek into unmapped territory and be supplied by air-drop. It was on that trip that I was nearly killed by my own bearers. After Purari, my labour line had been repatriated to Port Moresby and I had been given ten new men to replace them. They were from the delta and they greatly feared going into this Kukuku area. One morning, far away from anywhere, I called them to line up for the day's briefing. After getting no answer to a second call, I went to their hut. They were very sulky and rebellious. I shouted at them in the style which I had normally adopted, threatening them with some kind of penalty for not obeying. In a few minutes I was in a fight. It was a pandemonium of shouting and shoving. I reached for a stick and saw out of the corner of my eye a man picking up an axe. I yelled, 'No! that is a killing thing!' That frantic call must have touched something because the fight stopped and order was restored. I was never able to work with those men again and was given a new group at Mena.

Coming out of the Mena area later, instead of retracing our steps, we cut across country to the upper reaches of the Purari. Here we built large balsawood rafts. We then erected a framework with a canvas tent-fly roof and tied our belongings and stores securely in place. Launched out into the rapid water, it was the adventure of a lifetime. For three days we were swept along by the current, at first through rapids, then into the wider river, often spending hours paddling our way out of huge, slowly-circulating whirlpools or poling off sandbars. On the second day heavy rains upstream scoured the banks and brought huge trees into the river to become a hazard as they floated swiftly beside us. We tied up at night and slept on land above the flood level.

The swamps of the delta were not such fun. In fact they must be one of the worst places on earth. There was no dry land. It was a jungle of spiky sago palms growing in brackish water. All the worst of the stinging biting insects were there and the humidity was stifling. We could move only by cutting down trees to form floating pathways. We were constantly wet, either from slipping off the logs or from the endless pouring rain. Luckily my contract came to an end after a month in that area.

Now I had saved enough money to go to England, I returned home for a short holiday and then boarded the *Himalaya* to London, prepared to obtain a higher engineering qualification through the Institution of Civil Engineers.

...

On the ship to England there was a woman who, having noticed my surname on the passenger list, told me that my sister Tess was in London working as a journalist for a group of Australian newspapers. I had not seen or heard of Tess since our father died in 1934 and in fact, my being so young at the time, I did not remember anything about her. Soon after arrival I contacted her and we hit it off immediately. Tess knew London well and together we went in search of paintings by our reputed ancestors, of which there were a number in Hampton Court and the National Portrait Gallery in London.

It was not only a pleasure to meet Tess, but it was also very fortunate for me that I did. Soon after arrival in London I began to feel weak in the afternoons. Before long I was staying in my bed sweating with fever and slightly delirious. Tess arranged for a doctor, who diagnosed that I had a severe attack of malaria. He sent me to hospital. Without her attention, I may have had serious complications.

It turned out that I had picked up the disease from the mosquitos in Papua, but it only became virulent in my system weeks after I stopped taking the prophylactic pills. By the time I was admitted to hospital I was extremely anaemic, with my blood count down to sixtyfive percent of normal. Although cases of malaria were very rare in UK, my doctor happened to have worked in Africa and knew the symptoms. I was placed in the tropical diseases section of London University Hospital, where I became a showpiece for the students, who came in groups to see my extended spleen. Drugs were available and in two weeks my red cell count was restored and the parasite eradicated from my system. I never had a recurrence.

At twentyone, although I had come to London to extend my engineering qualifications, I was soon caught up in the fascination of new places. Travelling by ship I had seen the exotic port cities of Colombo, Bombay, Port Said, Aden, and Marseilles. Although I started to study engineering as an external student at Kings College, London University, in Bloomsbury, after four months I set out to travel around Europe. I spent the remainder of the year largely hitch-hiking and staying at Youth Hostels, in France, Italy, Austria and Germany. I met Tess briefly in Paris, where she introduced me to some of the more famous landmarks and places. I then followed the guide book highlights—the Loire Valley with its innumerable châteaux, the Riviera, Rome, Pompeii and Capri. I returned through Umbria to Florence and Venice, then crossed the Dolomite mountains to Innisbruck.

Europe was still recovering from the war and visas were needed at all borders. Few people hitch-hiked, although it was safe. Local people showed an interest in meeting an Australian. In Germany I joined a goodwill project of foreign students working together in the forest of the Harz Mountains with German young people.

Some had been Hitler Youth and were anxious to rehabilitate after the disorientation of defeat. I was then invited to stay in Hamburg with the German who was sponsoring the project. He was count but, like everyone else at that time, had lost all his wealth with the issue of new currency, but he still had a beautiful apartment and maintained the refinement of his class.

Back in London from France in August 1950, having spent all my savings in Europe, it was obvious that I would have to work and study part-time. Living in digs in South London, I took a job for a few months at Liberty's in Regent Street replying to customers' letters but, as winter came on, I found it too difficult to also keep up my studies. Through the Institution of Civil Engineers I found there was a possibility of an external course and of going out to Africa with the Colonial Service. I joined the Electricity Corporation of Nigeria (ECN) under the chief engineer Mr CU Jessup and sailed on the *Apapa* for Lagos on 15 November 1950.

I lived and worked three years in Nigeria. The salary and working conditions were good and, as it turned out, so was the social life.

The ECN had taken over operation of the Government electricity undertakings in 1951. At that time the consumption of electricity per head was only 4 kWh per year. The equipment in the oil and coal power stations was in a poor state often breaking down. It had been hoped that a cheap supply of power could be provided by developing the country's water resources, chiefly the Niger River and rivers in the Cameroon Highlands.

Initially I was junior engineer for general civil works and when I returned for a second term I was in charge of hydro-electric investigations. I was given the responsibility to arrange my own work program, ranging over a country one and a half times the size of France and with a population of more than thirty million people. I was equipped with a Land Rover and boat and travelled throughout the river systems, collecting information on stream flows at Ogun Gorge, Oni Gorge, Gurara Falls, Cross River and many other sites.

The countryside ranged from savannah with stunted trees over large areas to tropical forests in the south-east and semi-deserts in the north. Although West Africa was not so well endowed with large wild animals as East and Southern Africa, there were animals of some kind in all the remote areas. Where I camped on the Ogun, tribes of baboons would sit and watch me working. There I saw the extraordinary aardvark—a primitive mammal anteater like a huge pig. West Africa's most dangerous animal, the bush buffalo, left its tracks close to my camp one night.

With consultants from UK, I measured current speeds in rapids on the Niger River and explored the Bamenda Province in Eastern Nigeria, a remote and beautiful plateau where Fulani people lived virtually unvisited by outsiders. I spent some time in Victoria, near Cameroon, setting up gauging stations on a series of waterfalls in the dense jungle. The British had established a high standard of civil administration in this, their largest colony in Africa, and with it had set up a network of good rest houses. Using these, I travelled throughout Nigeria, working with the people in all three regions, visiting the highlands and meeting some northern chiefs. I prepared designs for large (barrage) and small (run-of-river) hydro-electric projects, the Niger River at Jebba being the most promising.

Just as I had a dangerous moment in Papua, I also got into trouble one day on the Oji River near Enugu. I started out to survey an area for a new power station and in order to clear a space where I could set up my theodolite, I set the grass alight, thinking that I could limit the fire. In a moment the wind swept the fire out of control and up the hillside towards a village. The fire was an enormous danger to the people's grass roof huts, threatening their children, their animals, and their granaries. There was panic as the whole village turned out to fight the flames. Luckily, they controlled it before it got to the houses. For a few moments I thought that I would be lynched. If the fire had reached their houses, I probably would have been. The village policeman suggested that I leave quietly and quickly. I was badly shaken and needed no convincing.

A village on the Niger River, Nigeria, West Africa

Meeting local chiefs with UK consultants, Northern Nigeria 1953

Nigeria was not yet fully independent from Great Britain in 1951 and the European expatriates still enjoyed many of the privileges of colonial living. Housing and cars were part of the salary package and everyone had servants. The tropical working day was short and social life was for most people the focus of their spare time. I played tennis and joined the yacht club, buying my own boat and spending weekends racing in the harbour and sailing to beautiful ocean beaches nearby. There were few single English women, but one , who was an ECN secretary, became a close friend. We sailed together, played tennis and enjoyed classical music. When it came to eating out and dancing, there were two clubs where Europeans could go on weekends. We got in with a crowd of BOAC (British Airways) pilots and joined their hectic party life.

After three years I completed my course by correspondence with BIET (affiliated with London University) in the UK, and passed the examinations for Associate Membership of the Institution of Civil Engineers (AMICE). I returned to London by ship in October 1953.

I now went to Paris to study the history of art. I took lodgings with a French professor of English on the Left Bank and began a systematic study of the galleries. I had been introduced to Mme Tanaka, widow of the Japanese artist, Tanaka. The American-born Mme Tanaka was in her eighties and with her husband, had been part of the group of artists including Picasso, Matisse, and Braque, who gathered in the cafes of Montparnasse in her earlier years. She was an enchanting personality, she knew the galleries well and had a fine artistic eye. Over the next three months I went with her regularly to all the galleries and exhibitions, examining, comparing and discussing the paintings from the Renaissance to the Moderns. I studied the history of the various movements and spent hours at her studio—stacked with Tanaka's gentle paintings—drinking coffee and listening to her stories of the famous artists and their agents, for whom she had mixed respect. 'Picasso owed much of his fame to his good agent,' she said.

Meantime I enjoyed the cafe life of the students. I had a French girlfriend, of whom I was very fond. She was a wine chemist and loved dancing. I think her parents were relieved when I left as they had a Gallic suspicion of the English, which extended to me.

Such had been my life when I encountered the writings of Ouspensky when travelling back from Europe to Australia in March 1954.

In Melbourne I returned to my parent's house. I took a job with one of the well-known firms of consulting engineers designing concrete structures, but my mind was elsewhere. I was obsessed by the implications of the Gurdjieff ideas: I could only hope to stay *awake* if I could find an esoteric school. For the time being I was simply earning a living.

When winter came I decided to go for a skiing weekend at Mt Hotham. I had brought a car with me from West Africa so I was able to drive up on the Friday night and the next morning enjoy myself on the snow. That evening as I sat with others around the large open fire in the chalet an attractive girl with her leg in plaster came in on crutches. I was introduced and spent a pleasant evening talking with her. We arranged to meet again back in Melbourne.

Ann lived in Balwyn only two kilometres from East Kew and I began to see her often at her parents' house. We were in love and soon became engaged. The following summer we were married. Ann's mother had a business that designed beautiful clothes. Her clients were the rich and famous. Our wedding was held in a fashionable church and the reception was, so the papers said, one of the most elegant that Melbourne had seen in those days.

I had told Ann about the Gurdjieff ideas. With her agreement I rang Coombe Springs and asked Mr Bennett if we could join his school. Apparently he thought that if we would travel half way around the world to attend, then we should be given a chance.

We decided to spend our honeymoon in India. We took a ship to Bombay and from there travelled across the country by train to Calcutta, and then on to Darjeeling. We stayed on a tea plantation with a young couple I had met the year before on the boat to Australia. Their house was on the high point of the estate and had a wide view of the Himalayas. We climbed Tiger Hill to watch the sunrise on the Kangchenjunga Range, met Sherpa Tensing (who had climbed Mount Everest with Edmund Hillary) and visited Sikkem, the nearest point in India to Tibet. On our way back we went sightseeing in Benares, then to Agra to see the Taj Mahal, and to Jaipur and Udaipur to see the water palaces of the Moguls. Three weeks later we picked up a ship at Bombay for London to start our new adventure at Coombe Springs.

~

Chapter Four

Subud at Coombe Springs

The day after my meeting with Mr Bennett at Coombe Springs, I went up to London and was shown into the large oak-panelled office of Mr William F Rees, in Victoria Street, SWI. (Victoria Street was to civil engineers what Harley Street was to doctors). As founder and managing director of the substantial company of building and civil engineering contractors bearing his name he was at the top of his profession. He greeted me with a friendly smile and fatherly touch on the arm. It was obvious by the way he spoke about my aunt that he was a close friend. After asking about my work experience and particular interests, he offered me a job in his company's project office in Norwich.

I returned to Coombe Springs and told Mr B what had happened. He said that there was a small group of Gurdjieff people in Norwich meeting under the leadership of Dr Brian Jennings, a psychiatrist. We could join them and, as Norwich was only a hundred miles away, that we could drive down each weekend for the *Y Group* meetings. I took the job and moved to Norwich that same week.

Brian and Mary Jennings became our mentors and the source of our daily Gurdjieff self-knowledge exercises. The basis was the writings of Ouspensky, which I continued to read: Firstly the admission (which I had come to) that man does not know *himself.* He is in fact a machine brought into motion by reacting. As he is, everything just happens to him. However, he can know that he is mechanical and then he may find ways to change. He must realise that *he* is not one; not one unchanging *I,* he is many. (His body, his name, and his habits give him the illusion of always being the same.)

'Development,' Ouspensky wrote, 'cannot begin until man realises that he does not possess the qualities that he ascribes to himself: capacity to do, permanent ego, consciousness and will.'

Observation of our ourselves, he said, leads us to the conclusion that man is not conscious of himself, but man has the possibility of four states of consciousness: *sleep, waking state, self-consciousness* and *objective consciousness.* He lives only in the first two states: sleep and waking state. Our waking state might be more accurately called 'waking sleep' or 'relative consciousness'. Of this I was convinced.

We rented a flat and set up our first home. We drove the three and a half hour journey to Coombe Springs each weekend. After two long days of heavy manual work in the garden I would return so tired on Sunday night that I would fall asleep at the wheel. We only made it by Ann sharing the driving those long hours after midnight on the deserted roads.

Winter brought its share of snow and rain and long evenings by a small briquette fire. The WF Rees office in Norwich had been established for a large contract in the area so when, after Christmas, our tender was unsuccessful it was decided to close. Mr Rees sent a message to say that the only job he had available for me was on Jersey, in the Channel Islands. This wouldn't permit us to continue attending the Gurdjieff group so I resigned. Mr B said if we came back to London we could live at Coombe Springs in the *Fish Bowl.*

I now took a job as a design engineer with Soil Mechanics Ltd, the consulting division of John Mowlem and Company, one of England's four main contractors. The office was in Victoria Street. Ann learnt to type and also went out to work. As winter lingered on, the London fogs—it was the days of London's infamous smog—were so thick that, if we used the car, one of us would have to walk in front to keep us on the road.

Now in residence we became immersed in the 'secret society' atmosphere of Coombe Springs, devoting ourselves daily to the psychological exercises designed to awaken us from our sleeping state and to establishing a more permanent waking consciousness.

Mr Bennett was the leader for the residents' special group and, although I would not have thought in those terms at the time, he was a father figure to me. I loved, admired and trusted him. He was the finest man—in terms of his humanity, intelligence and value system—that I had ever met. He became an important influence in my life for which I was to remain forever grateful.

I was totally committed to *The Work,* as the Gurdjieff system was called. It was said that inner work must proceed on three levels: for oneself, for the group, and for mankind. I had no problem in honouring this, as I was convinced of my own need and that mankind needed conscious people. As for the group level, the feeling of brotherhood among the Gurdjieff people surpassed anything I had ever known.

Living at Coombe Springs was, for me, a wonderful experience. The rituals of 5.00 am cold water ablutions in winter to midnight saunas only reinforced my zeal. I was young, strong and healthy. We practised sensing exercises—through relaxation and attention; self observation —through acts of self denial, and the movements. All these produced higher quality energies and improved awareness. Not that self-knowledge was always a happy experience. When I found that I couldn't experience the sensation of my limbs in the relaxation exercises I was very frustrated. As time passed, I found that my quality of perception improved and I had glimpses of a more intense experience of reality. For example, after a weekend of concentration, I would see the actual *being* of my environment that I had passed a hundred times before, seeing it only as objects. A tree seen with this higher energy became a living being, with a *presence.* Ouspensky might have called such modest experiences 'Living on pennies found in the street—a poor standard of living', but to me it gave my life aim and direction. As a young pupil I had so much to learn from Mr Bennett that the bigger question of whether the Gurdjieff system could ultimately bring me to a permanent change of being rather than to a temporary change of perception never bothered me.

In August 1956 Ann and I went for a holiday to France. Mr Bennett arranged for us to meet the leader of a Gurdjieff group in Paris on the way. The teacher was Tchekhovitch, a Russian émigré, who had been with Gurdjieff before he died in 1941. All I knew about him was from a story told by Mr B that he was a huge man (he had been a wrestler as a young man) and that one day when he was with Gurdjieff he had fallen asleep with exhaustion while working high up on a scaffolding. The other students had the job of getting him down.

We had been invited to arrive at 9 pm at a small upstairs flat in a poor district of central Paris. (It may have been the flat used by Gurdjieff himself.) We didn't know that there would be a meeting and there had been no mention of a meal. In England our dinner was at 6 pm. We therefore had something to eat—not just a snack but a substantial steak dinner. When we arrived we found a narrow room almost filled by a long table. Several people were preparing food in a kitchenette. Everyone was, in the Gurdjieff fashion, going about their business in total silence. More people arrived and more food was placed on the table. There was seating for about eight but the food looked enough for thirty. Every dish was different from any I had seen before—soused fish, goulash, a very special red beet and herb salad, and so on. Finally we sat down and we were toasted as guests and invited to eat. Taking only a little, I was pressed to take more. The next hour was agony. I had to keep eating because every dish was served and I was a guest. I never forgot my lesson: when invited out, be prepared to honour the host's hospitality. After the meal came the mental exercises. They were like mathematical puzzles with a twist. Tchekhovitch would ask questions, going around the room person by person. Not speaking French, I thought I could escape this game, but no, the questions were translated. I didn't fare any better than I had with the food. When it finished in the late hours, I left unhappily aware of my shortcomings. The objective to show me my weaknesses had been successful. But what I remember more than the shame was the extraordinary feeling of love from the big Russian as he walked us down the dark wet cobblestone street, his arms enveloping us like an huge bear.

At Mr B's suggestion we went to visit the Château du Prieurè, Avon, near Fontainebleau, where Gurdjieff had located his school before the war. Now used as a nursing home, its grounds neglected, it was hard to imagine the intensity of life that filled its halls and gardens in the days of Katherine Mansfield. From there we went south to see the pre-historic paintings discovered this century at Lascaux in France and those in Altamira in Spain. Mr B had visited these caves with Gurdjieff who, he said, had interpreted the mysterious composite animal as being an emblem of an esoteric society, and the deer as totems of individual people, the number of points on the antlers representing the degree of attainment.

After almost a year living at Coombe Springs we joined with four other families to buy and convert Beverley Lodge, a large Edwardian house nearby in Coombe Lane, into apartments. It had great oak trees and, in spring, drifts of bluebells and daffodils.

I had meantime joined the Coombe Springs architects' group on the design of a new *movements* hall called the Djamichunatra (a Gurdjieff word relating to the transformation process, later shortened by popular use to the Djami) and became responsible for the structural engineering design. The group of twelve professionals worked together with Mr B to develop a building with an atmosphere appropriate to its sacred use such as Mr B had seen during his travels in the Middle East. The proportions were calculated according to the symbolism of the Gurdjieff *Enneagram,* a mystical symbol portraying the transformation of man's spiritual energies. We all believed the building was very special, both for its aesthetic design and for its symbolism. Mr Bennett's record of the design and building of the Djamichunatra is described in his book *Witness.* He writes that on 15 September 1953 he went on a journey to South-west Asia:

> '... to make a study of the buildings old and new which had been used for various rituals and spiritual exercises by Christians, Muslims and the lesser sects of South-west Asia. My aim was to discover, if possible, the way in which enclosed spaces can concentrate psychic energies. My own studies had led me to the belief that the shape and size of buildings and the disposition of the masses have an effect upon the psychic state of those who enter them to share in an experience.

'In Istanbul, I went out of the old city through the Adrianople Gate, and found the monastery of the Mevlevi dervishes which I used to visit in 1920. ... I measured the Sema Hané and made sketches. Later, I did the same at the Mevlevi Hané in Péra, now a police station, and found that the basic dimensions were identical.

'On the 22 September I travelled to Konya. ... Every day that I spent in Konya I went to the great Mevlevi Tekke, the home of the poet Djellaluddin Rumi—founder of the Order of Mevlevi Dervishes. The Sema Hané was built in the twelfth century under the direction of his son, Sultan Veled, by the Seldjuk Kings of Konya. It is the prototype of three hundred and sixty-five similar buildings, distributed throughout South-west Asia. As I studied it, I became convinced that the size and proportions of the building were derived from some lost art of creating a concentration of psychic energies, that could influence the inner state of those who met in it to worship God.

On 11 May 1955, Mr Bennett went for a two week trip to Baghdad and Damascus where a dervish teacher told him that 'a Messenger is already on earth ... to show the way (out of the present great wickedness in the world) and that he (Mr Bennett) was one of those chosen to prepare the way.' He then writes:

'Within fifteen days of leaving London, I was back again at Coombe Springs. Two decisions had been taken. I would propose to the Council of the Institute that we should go forward with the building of a great hall at Coombe Springs, and I would give a series of public lectures in London in the autumn. The group of architects, under the leadership of Robert Whiffen, was delighted with the decision to build. The money was made available by loans made by our pupils in amounts from one pound to two thousand. A new life seemed to inspire Coombe Springs.

'On 23rd March, 1956 ... (we) started work on the great hall. Snow was on the ground as we worked. As the weeks passed, we were surrounded by crocuses, daffodils and bluebells. The team formed itself. In addition to English residents at Coombe, we had Americans, Canadians, Australians, South Africans and a Norwegian. Whenever a specialist was needed, he appeared from somewhere. The work of the architects' group was out of the ordinary. Twelve to fifteen men, with sharply differing tastes and views on architecture, worked together without either pay or personal credit. 'No single feature was incorporated in the building that all did not accept. This sometimes meant waiting for weeks or months before some part of the building could go forward.

I took some part in all this, but we were all convinced that no one person could do anything. The building seemed to have a plan and a purpose of its own, and all we could do was to wait until one part after another of the plan was revealed.

'We had laid out the hall so that the central axis pointed to Fontainebleau where Gurdjieff was buried. He had spoken of a nine-sided building which exemplified in its proportions the Laws of World Creation and World Maintenance, and as the plan of the new hall came to life, we found in it an expression of the laws of which Gurdjieff wrote in *All and Everything*. ... I was asked to give a name to the building, and chose the word Djamichunatra, taken from Chapter 46 of *All and Everything*, where it is used to describe the place where the soul receives its spiritual nourishment.'

In March 1956 at Mr B's suggestion I gave up my work with Mowlem's in London to supervise the construction. He arranged for me to have the conservatory in the main house as an office. When we came to start we found that we had all the skills necessary within the membership. Largely they were capable amateurs and included carpenters from among the architects, a hobby welder, a plumber trained in copper roofing, and a sculptor. A stained glass artist, Rosemary Rutherford, was a professional. A small team worked during the week and up to forty on the weekends.

As part of *The Work* Mr B made everything as difficult as possible. We had to dig and screen our own gravel for the concrete from within the grounds. At first he insisted we build a crane instead of hiring one. When this proved dangerous and unworkable, he allowed us to hire one, but only on condition that we erected it ourselves piece by piece. Our trust was exceeded only by our sincerity and commitment. We worked physically until we almost dropped from exhaustion and then continued on with our psychological exercises. We forged a brotherhood through sacrifice and common desperation—the need to *remember ourselves.* Every detail was constructed with loving care. Scrolls containing information about *The Work* were sealed into the large redwood frames for posterity.

In appearance the building shape was unique and striking. It had nine sides with large slanting cedar walls rising from a fifteen metres diameter concrete base. It stood twenty metres high with a sloping faceted roof. Inside, subdued light filtered down through slots in the top of the walls, and three large stained glass windows high up on the timber walls lit the space above. There was no furniture except for a seat for about eighty people around the inside perimeter. The timber floor was covered with rugs for large meetings. Although the building did not appear large from the outside, the height and vaulting ceiling inside created a sense of inner space. Even with three hundred people seated it did not seem crowded.

We were delighted when Frank Lloyd Wright, whose wife had connections with the Gurdjieff movement in the USA, came to see it and gave his approval. 'A nice little building!' he said.

Architects: Left background Richard Bigwood and right Bob Whiffen

Djamichunatra meeting in the Conservatory, Coombe Springs,1956

Architects' meeting. John Donat left, myself centre right, Tom Pope right

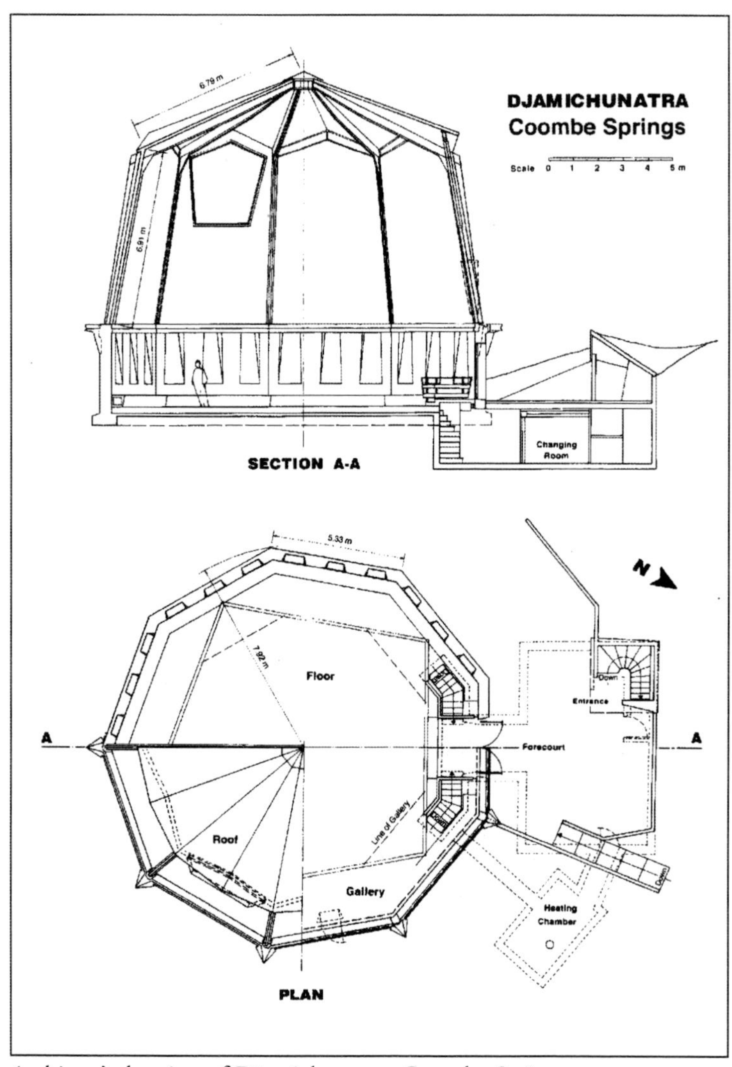

Architect's drawing of Djamichunatra, Coombe Springs

Djamichunatra construction, the nine main frames in position

Inspecting the roof framing. Bob Prestie on the right. Photos John Donat

Placing the Djamichunatra frames. Bob Whiffen (left) and John Blakey

Djamichunatra construction continued late into the night

Djamichunatra completed in autumn 1957. Photo John Donat

Djamichunatra in the winter snow 1957

Frank Lloyd Wright inspects the Djamichunatra 1957. Photo John Donat

An Experiment in Modern Living

by
JESSICA
YOUNG

Five families share an Edwardian house in Kingston-upon-Thames

FIVE FAMILIES, all close friends, who wanted a home near London, have worked out a novel solution to the housing problem. They found a large Edwardian house, Beverley Lodge, Kingston-upon-Thames, pooled their resources and bought it between them. The house could have only two legal owners, but, in practice, each of the five contributed according to the floor space they intended to occupy. As only one or two of the flats had "usual offices," each was equipped with kitchen and bathroom fittings from the common money pool.

After two years, the participators report that they are still the best of friends and, far from finding themselves at too close quarters, they all live quite independent lives and are delighted when they meet away from home. A courageous experiment in mutual confidence, and a most successful one. Our photographs show three of the five homes.

THE JAPANESE FLAT

Although separated by only one floor from Mrs. King's Dutch flat, one seems in walking upstairs to have travelled half-way across the earth. Jan van Sommers is a constructional engineer with a family background of interest in design, and he and his wife, Ann, were inspired by Japan for the appearance of their beautiful modern flat. Its decor is almost all white, with natural pine boarding used everywhere for its feeling of cleanness and for its simplicity.

In the hall an African carpet in ochre, black and white sets the colour scheme, the ceiling being painted ochre. A lino-cut by Mr. van Sommers' father has an African theme.

Leading straight through from the hall is the kitchen-dining-room, with a solid modern table and chairs of natural beech in the dining recess. The working surfaces in the kitchen and also the deep window recess in the living-room were all cut from a huge old kitchen table and match the mellow colour of the grooved-and-tongued pine boarding.

As the rooms were small, it was decided to keep them as free of furniture as possible. In the sitting-room, the floor space is empty, and guests are asked to remove their shoes before entering, for they will sit on brightly coloured cushions on the white Indian carpet. A divan with a vividly striped cover is available for those who need more support! Ground-level bookcases and plenty of prints on the wall banish any sense of austerity in this tranquil, beautiful room.

Top: for the Japanese living-room colour was limited to blue curtains, a striped divan cover, bright cushions against white walls and white carpet.

Left: the kitchen shows Japanese influence in its use of natural wood with white walls and a sunny, yellow floor — simple, practical and spotless.

Left: the hall of Mr. and Mrs. van Sommers' Japanese flat. Light is admitted from the staircase through a large plate-glass panel wall.

The van Sommers' flat conversion in Beverley Lodge, near Coombe Springs

In early 1957, as the hall was nearing completion, Mr B told us, in the 'Young Group', that something important was going to happen. He said no more, except that it was confidential. In the weeks that followed I began to experience a deep remorse. It was not a feeling of self-judgment about any specific error. It was more a general and overwhelming heavy feeling that I was altogether less than I ought to be. When I told Mr B's wife Elizabeth, she said, 'I believe that what you are experiencing is connected with something important that is coming.'

About this time Mr B told us that he had come to believe that the prospects for any of us ever reaching a change of *essence* through the Gurdjieff teaching were extremely limited. However, he said, a man has now come who can help us. He believed that this person had been foretold in Gurdjieff's writings as the one who could open the conscience of man. He said very little else about what to expect.

What we were to learn later was that this help involved a completely new and different process where, instead of us relying on a spiritual teacher and our own efforts, we would be brought into contact with a tangible higher power, or life force. And that by surrendering to this higher power, the higher power itself would work the transformation of our essence or soul. This power, moreover, had only newly become available to mankind, and was a gift from God brought by the one sent to transmit it, Pak Subuh, who had founded the *Subud* brotherhood for this purpose.

Before telling us, Mr B had himself received the contact with this higher power and had been *opened** in Subud. As I had been doing relaxation exercises in a group with him every day, I had been exposed to its working, known as the *latihan,* and it was this, I later came to understand, that had stirred my conscience.

Soon afterwards Bapak Muhammad Subuh (Pak Subuh) arrived at Coombe Springs.

* For the meaning of this and other Subud terms, *see* **Subud Glossary** .

On 7 June 1957 I joined a small group of about six men to be *opened* by Pak Subuh in Mr Bennett's study in Coombe Springs. As I entered the darkened room—the only light was filtered through the drawn blinds—I didn't immediately see the figures already there. The air was warm and smelt of some aromatic spice, which I later found to be the clove cigarettes smoked by the Indonesians. I had taken off my shoes and was aware of the carpet underfoot. Then I saw Pak Subuh and with him Mr B and one or two others. We were told to close our eyes and relax. I stood quietening myself with all the piety that I could command.

Then Pak Subuh said 'Begin!'. Nearby I heard movement and sighs, and sensed, or perhaps imagined, he was in front of me. I felt my consciousness draining away and fell as if in a faint. I came to as someone said 'Finish!' and I saw that others were also on the floor or starting to get up.

Three days later I repeated the *latihan,* again with Bapak (as Pak Subuh was known) and a group of other men who had also been opened. We were told to close our eyes and follow whatever arose from within us, and to take no notice of other people. As soon as Bapak said 'Begin!' I could hear activity and sounds all around me. Some people were moving about, some letting out cries, some laughing with relief, and so on. It was not easy to ignore the noise but as no one actually bumped into me I gradually relaxed and followed the slight indications of movement that I seemed to feel. That week there was a constant procession of new people coming to Coombe Springs to receive the *contact* from Bapak. The atmosphere of expectation was intense.

The following week, on 14 June 1957, Bapak gave his first explanatory talk to newly-opened men and women at Coombe Springs. This was the first time that I had been able to observe Bapak. He was of medium height, taller than the other Indonesians in his party, and well built. He moved easily without haste or superfluous movement, giving the impression that he was completely at ease with himself and his surroundings. He was in his late fifties.

Bapak Muhammad Subuh at Coombe Springs, June 1957

He dressed neatly in a western suit and tie and wore an Islamic black velvet petji (a hat without a brim). His soft brown eyes were direct and steady, seeming to see much more than ordinary people do and yet friendly. He had a ready smile which showed perfect even white teeth against his smooth light brown skin. When he spoke he accompanied his rich voice with expressive gestures, his body moving with the eloquence of his words.

Bapak started by saying that his talk was only for those who had already been opened and were following the latihan. From this I understood that he wished to avoid anyone inadvertently being opened who had not freely asked for the contact. I quote him here at length as this explanation was my introduction to Subud:

'For those of you who are not yet opened it is not time for you to listen to this, for what Bapak is going to explain is more or less the direction and requirements of the spiritual way. Maybe one day you too can listen. According to Bapak's experience, it is not Bapak who would be harmed, but those listeners who have not yet received the training [latihan], since they still lack the inner strength to receive this. It might lead to unpleasant consequences, and if that happens they will certainly blame Bapak.

Brothers and sisters, all of you who are present here at this time, before Bapak explains what is needed and other matters related to the spirit, Bapak—as an ordinary human being who is always affected and enveloped by mistakes in his behaviour—does not forget to ask your forgiveness in case there is something in what he says that offends you, that hurts your feelings and makes you unhappy. That is what Bapak asks of you all.

As regards the training [latihan] that you have all received, is in truth the worship of the One God by human beings, but not in a way that is familiar to you, for Bapak can say that this training is something new that he has been willed by God to practise. But its content is not new: it was present at the beginning of everything, and it was recorded as the content of all those who have tried to worship the greatness of God.

'And why does this particular method differ from the others? Maybe because nowadays human beings are truly oppressed by the conditions of rapid progress that are taking place, and are unwilling, or find it hard to resist all the pressures that are continuously acting upon them. For human beings nowadays are no longer like those in earlier times who only experienced quietness and tranquillity; today human beings are confronted by conditions that are full of things that can harm and diminish their human status.

'This is perhaps why it is God's will that we should be able to practise our worship without neglecting or putting aside or withdrawing from the state of the world we face at this time. It is clear that, whatever it was that you received in your training [latihan], you remained fully conscious. The purpose or significance of this is that God indeed intends human beings to worship Him without withdrawing from or putting aside their normal needs in this world. So, in order to worship God you do not need to isolate yourself, avoid society or your worldly needs. You should be able to worship God while living a normal life, enjoying the companionship of your wife, children and friends.

'Indeed, this state or experience you have received is unexpected and also beyond the realm of the human intellect. It is also beyond human expectation that a teaching or practice or training that leads to the worship of God looks so simple and be practised while living the complete life of a normal human being. That is why there are very many people who consider—and say—that what we obtain in the training [latihan] cannot be true because we only practise it for such a very short time. In general, as Bapak himself found out, many of those who practise what Bapak called the worship of God or apply themselves to mystical ways, spend considerable amounts of time at it.

'Bapak does not find fault with these opinions, for indeed that is generally how it was done in the past. But the fact that Bapak has been able to receive, and in turn to guide you, by such a simple way, is fortunate for human beings in general. And perhaps this has happened because of the will of God who—if we thought of God as a human—

has remembered the state of mankind at this time. However, if Bapak examines the state of the world—and God's response to it—more deeply and more broadly, it becomes clear that [what we have received] is indeed well suited to our time or our epoch and works in a way that fits with today.

'In fact, in times past something like this already existed, and was also received by the prophets; the reason why it was not practised is because at that time such a way was not needed. The present is different from those earlier times and those earlier times were very different from today. This is what Bapak needed to explain regarding the apparent difference between one and the other. ...'

At the end of his explanation Bapak answered questions.

Questioner:
'In us there is an attention that has to be fixed on something, or it will go into thoughts, feelings, or daydreams ... (What should we do about that?)'

Bapak:
That will come by itself, later, for this is from the power of God, so it can overcome any obstacle. Indeed, it is an attribute of the human brain that it must think, therefore it is not possible for you to quieten your thoughts until your brain has been separated from your self: God will not take it away but He is able to reach through it. So the part of the brain that thinks will continue to think, but the way in which it thinks will be different. For previously it was filled with desire (in Indonesian nafsu) and eventually it will be filled with the power of God. That's how it works.

Take something that is easy to see, like walking. You may have seen or experienced it yourself in the training (latihan), that you are trained to walk, even though you clearly already know how to walk, since you are already accustomed to walking. But with the latihan your walk is different from your normal walk. When you are walking with the latihan you may feel, 'This is very strange; I am walking even though I have no desire to walk.'

What this shows is that the power of God is there before every beginning. Thus the steps you take after having received the latihan can eventually be a guidance that will save your own feet, for your feet will no longer be able to get lost.

For example, once these legs have been filled (with God's power), they spontaneously turn away. You experience the same thing in your training (latihan) when you are walking like this and there is a friend in front of you, you turn around by yourself. Clearly the inner part of you knows more than the outer. In Dutch they call it instinctlief.

[Recording 57 CSP 1]

As to the origin of the *latihan*, I first read about it in the book *Concerning Subud,* which Mr Bennett wrote in 1959:

'Bapak was born near Semarang in Central Java, on 22 June 1901, a date which coincided with the birthday of the Prophet Muhammad on the Islamic calendar. The baby was named Sukarno but with that name he was always ill so it was changed to Muhammad Subuh, to correspond with the time of his birth, 5 am—Subuh,* meaning dawn. He was raised by his grandparents. At school he was taught in Javanese and Indonesian, and later in the Dutch language. When his grandfather died Bapak took a job and studied book-keeping, taking over the care of his parents and younger brother and sister.

'One night in Semarang in the summer of 1925, when he was twenty-four years of age, he received the latihan. He had gone out for a walk and at about 1 am on his way home he was startled by a light shining from above. He looked up to see a ball of radiant white light fall on his head. His body started shaking, and his chest heaving. He hurried home and lying on his bed he surrendered to God. He then arose, but not from his own will, and performed his Islamic prayers. From then on he was woken almost every night and made to move: martial arts, dancing, singing new melodies, and so on.

'In the years that followed many friends interested in spiritual matters used to regularly visit Bapak's house to seek advice.

* Subuh: The word Subuh has no direct connection with the word Subud.

He continued to receive and follow these movements of his inner self which he later called the *latihan kejiwaan* and, although these people came in contact with the life force that he was receiving, Bapak said he felt that it was not yet the time to open people. …

'During 1932 he had a number of strong spiritual experiences and as a result he felt it necessary to give up work in order to devote himself totally to the latihan. The confirmation to do this came around the time of his birthday in June with his experience of a spiritual Ascension. He then understood that it was his mission and his task to transmit to everyone who asked for it the latihan that he had received. …

'During World War II, he moved to Yogyakarta and by 1945 there were about three hundred people following the latihan. He gave the group the name *Susila Budhi Dharma*, or SUBUD for short.'

…

For the months after my opening, the latihan was everything. Every day it was my preoccupation. Every latihan I wondered at my good fortune. In the Djami, and later in a large wooden hut, at various times I ran or shook, I wept or laughed, I shouted or sang, I felt my breathing change and stop, I prayed and felt deep silence. Outside I was occasionally touched with blissful joy. I remember sitting in the sun in the rose garden marvelling at everything around me, too beautiful to be expressed in words. The overall effect was inner peace and certainty about the latihan.

My earliest advice from Bapak came during this time when, soon after I was opened, he entered my office where I was working on the construction program for the Djami. He looked at the bar charts showing the building activities in sequence with connecting lines and arrows and said simply, in English, 'Right work!'

The impact of this was, not so much to reassure me that I had chosen the most suitable calling, as this had never been a question for me, but rather to establish a personal relationship with him.

Bapak and his wife Ibu at Coombe Springs, summer 1957

Bapak giving a talk in the Djamichunatra:
(left to right) Ibu, Sjafrudin, Bapak, Icksan Ahmad and John Bennett

The scene outside the front door of Coombe Springs at Bapak's arrival:
(front, left to right) Anwar and Ratna Zakir, Éva Bartok

Then pointing to my chest he said (through his interpreter), 'You were lucky to receive the latihan, otherwise you get sick in there.' I was quite healthy at the time, so this was clearly insight about a weakness. Perhaps because my father had died of pulmonary TB? As my latihan progressed I sometimes breathed heavily, and more than once my breathing stopped for a short period. Again Bapak's assurance that the latihan was of value to me was unnecessary, instead the effect was to consolidate my feeling of connection with Bapak.

As the weeks passed I began to experience doubt about myself. I could not 'find myself'; I felt I had no *I*. My mind found me wanting in every way. It said that I could not relax enough, I could not surrender enough. I was outside God's love. I had never doubted like this in my life. This was my first experience of purification. The problem of *I* which was central to the Gurdjieff work had, by my efforts at concentrating my will on the question, built or crystallised an inner attitude to the problem of identity. Now this attitude was being worked on by the latihan. The unseen concerns which I had accumulated by the Gurdjieff work and which had become imprinted in my psyche were now becoming apparent on their way out. This might be compared with the notion that 'at death our whole life passes before our eyes'. My surrender of my will to God's Will in the latihan was causing a death of these concerns.

One day Ichsan, Bapak's translator, saw me in this state. 'Come! we walk,' he said, sweeping me up with his smile. We walked arm in arm in the garden. 'Just feel,' he laughed, 'You (are) relaxed!' Gradually over the weeks I became accustomed to my doubting and to my ever-changing thoughts. I was all of them—all these *I's*— and, as I gave my attention to other things, my peace returned.

On 3 November 1957 the Djamichunatra was formally offered to Subud. In his inauguration talk Bapak said not to attach undue importance to a building, a reminder of how involved we had become. Mr B rewarded my efforts by paying for an overseas holiday.

We chose to go to Morocco, flying to Gibraltar and crossing to Tangier by boat. Through Husein Rofé, who at that time was coming to latihan at Coombe Springs, we arranged to stay in a small hotel owned by friends of his, the Buckinghams. Husein was an Englishman who was opened by Bapak in Java in 1950 and subsequently played a key role in the spread of Subud outside Indonesia. He brought the contact to England and opened Mr Bennett in November 1956. The Buckinghams were Americans who had lived many years in Tangier. When we arrived I noticed that they were well-known in the Moslem community. They sent out plates of food regularly to the needy and were greeted by the locals wherever they went. As we walked down the street with them we were invited to take tea and cake with the shopkeepers who sat on low rug-covered platforms at the back of their stalls.

Tangier was small and exotic in those days. The hotel, in a long-established area of good quality houses, was built in a beautiful location on a steep cliff that overlooked the Atlantic. The winding narrow streets of the district were bordered by whitewashed walls hung with bougainvillea. The Buckinghams treated us more as friends of Husein than as paying guests, taking us sightseeing and out to restaurants at their expense.

We went inland by train to Fez and Meknes in the foothills of the Atlas Mountains. The intensity of Gurdjieff work during the months in UK, and probably the effect of the latihan (although I was not yet conscious its effects), heightened the quality of my seeing. I was spellbound as I watched the spectrum of pinks and purples of the desert in the changing afternoon light and the awesome canopy of brilliant stars at night. There were few tourists and most local people living in the old town streets and markets appeared to us to be following a life unchanged from medieval times. We visited the markets and the colourful wool-dying area. Berbers, tall and straight, every face etched with character, could be seen dressed in their traditional long handwoven robes. The serenity of these people seemed to us proof of the effectiveness of their Islamic religion.

In the spring of 1958 Bapak returned to Indonesia. Before he went he appointed emergency helpers to take care of the hundreds of people now attending latihan. I was one and had the added task of corresponding with members who had returned to their homelands.

Meantime I had written to my mother about Coombe Springs and in the summer she travelled from Australia to stay with us at Beverley Lodge. She said later that she had hoped to join Subud, but when she got there it somehow didn't work out. I don't know what happened. Perhaps I didn't handle it well. On her way home to Australia she had a severe heart attack. This was later followed by a stroke and some paralysis. In fact my mother was never without illness from that time on. She bore her disabilities with courage, constantly occupying herself weaving, producing beautiful and intricate designs for table linen. She was opened later.

On 18 December 1958 we joined Husein Rofé in Malta for a holiday. A mutual woman friend from Coombe Springs was also visiting there. We all lodged at the same small hotel on the waterfront, where we stayed five days, talking a lot and making excursions together over the rocky fields. Our friend was considering living permanently on the island, and planned to make an income by painting and pottery. She was anxious about her future and we were at times worried by her emotional state.

As it approached Christmas we left Husein in Malta and moved on to Assisi in Italy. We had hardly arrived before I started to quarrel violently with Ann, something that I had almost never done. I was angry beyond measure and stormed off up a grassy hill saying that I was going to leave her.

I had so little experience of the latihan that I did not realise that I was going through a strong purification. It seems that I had picked up our friend's anxiety in Malta and it was coming out on my wife. *It must out* had been an Indonesian saying at Coombe Springs, but now I didn't understand what was happening to me.

By Christmas Eve the experience had passed and we attended midnight Mass at the basilica of St Francis in Assisi. The church had three levels, an upper one where the frescoes of the life of St Francis attributed to Giotto were located, the main church at street level in the middle where services were held, and a crypt at the bottom with the tomb of St Francis. As it approached midnight and the church became packed to the doors with standing worshippers, I began to feel very oppressed, so much so that I had to push my way out through the crowd and leave as quickly as possible to avoid being overcome by the experience. Here again I didn't know enough about the latihan to realise what was happening.

Later I understood that forces activating people's moods can be transferred from one person to another without talking. Ideally, as the latihan cleans our *inner feeling,* we can know what is our own state and what force is coming to us from others, and also know how inwardly to separate from these forces. *Inner feeling* as used by Bapak in his explanations about the *latihan* has a particular meaning in Subud and is difficult to grasp, even after having been opened and having received the *latihan.* In writing about inner experiences, this problem is further complicated by the normal ambiguity of familiar words when applied to spiritual matters. For example the word *feeling* is used loosely by us in English to describe almost every experience: We say we *feel* hot or cold when we have a sensation, we say I *feel* you are right or wrong when we are actually making a thinking judgement, we use *feel* to describe a hunch which may be an intuition, and most commonly we talk about *feeling* angry or sad when we are describing an emotion. CG Jung limits the meaning of *feeling* to describe our function for making a judgement of value—for example, agreeable or disagreeable.

Inner feeling as used by Bapak has a different meaning. It refers to our experience of our inner self in the latihan state, when we are inwardly separated from our judgements, our emotions, and our opinions. It is therefore given a singular noun.

Sensitivity to the forces is needed for us in Subud in order to live according to guidance from the grace of God. As it was, I had begun to be sensitive but had no idea what was happening or how to handle the experience. As my experience in the church became overwhelming, I did the only thing possible—leave. Once outside, we went down to the crypt. It was empty, as everyone was attending the Mass. Now as I approached the sarcophagus containing the body of St Francis I felt myself become deeply peaceful. It was so immediate and clear, that I felt that I was experiencing the presence of the saint himself. With the peace came a sense of the holiness of this place. I left with gratitude and veneration for the saint.

In August 1959 Bapak returned to Coombe Springs to attend the First Subud World Congress. After the Djamichunatra was completed, I had returned to work with John Mowlem and Company where I was employed on the construction of the 33-storey Vickers-Armstrong building in London, and in the evenings I was assisting Niels Lisborg, lecturer at the Architectural Association, with the writing of his textbook *Structural Design.* Both jobs were interesting but for some reason I had become restless and uncertain about staying in England.

This time Bapak's guidance to me was more direct. I was among a small crowd of members waiting at the front door to see him arrive. As he began to walk from the car his eyes met mine and I felt at that moment that I would like to go to Indonesia and work with him. My lifelong commitment to Subud was born. During the following weeks, I asked his advice as to where Ann and I should live. He said New Zealand, but agreed that we first come to Indonesia.

On 26 May 1960, after Bapak had left England on his way to Indonesia, we sailed from Southampton aboard the *Willem Ruys* for Singapore, then flew to Jakarta.

~

Bapak and Mr. Bennett, Coombe Springs 1957-59

(left to right) Mariam Kibble, Ibu, Irena, Bapak, Icksan, Bob Prestie, Ismana

Delegates at the First Subud World Congress, Coombe Springs 1959

Temporary dining tent, Subud World Congress 1959, Coombe Springs

Chapter Five

Preparations for Cilandak

In 1960 Bapak lived in Jakarta at 68 Djalan Tjokroaminoto (also Jalan Jawa), Menteng. It was a single storey brick house in the same residential area as many of the foreign embassies. The streets were lined with large and colourful flame trees which shaded the sidewalks. It was an elegant and quiet suburb where the main road traffic was bicycle rickshaws.

Bapak welcomed me like a father, tolerant and encouraging to my willingness to help. He arranged our accommodation as his guests and I became an employee of Subud on a small retainer. He gave us the new names Lionel and Helena. It was not uncommon in Subud for people to change their first names. Although the practice was part of Indonesian-Islamic culture, in Subud it was a matter of choice, based on a person's feeling for the need to change. Bapak gave new names when asked and occasionally suggested a change. He once gave this explanation:

'There is no compulsion or obligation in Subud to change your name. It is up to you whether or not you wish to do so. However, a name does, in fact, have a strong influence on the self of man, because when a person is called by his name, he will certainly respond from his whole being, so that his entire self, when called by name, feels as if it is being awoken from sleep, or stirred out of passivity.

If a person or child is wrongly named, then when his inner feeling is awakened and rises, it becomes adjusted to a name which does not correspond to his inner self. As a result, his outer behaviour and his inner feeling are not in harmony.' [Recording 63 BCL 3]

First we lived with Bapak's son Haryono and his wife Ismana in their company-owned house, a few streets away from Bapak's home. They had one daughter Isti, from Ismana's former marriage. Haryono was an engineer and managing director of Logam Mulia, the government-owned gold refinery. As the only foreigners, we lived entirely within the Indonesian culture. I was flooded with new and exotic impressions—sights, sounds, smells, tastes, and feelings.

In August Bapak formally established the secretariat for the Subud Spiritual World Centre. Those appointed were his existing secretarial assistants, Sudarto Martohudojo, Brodjolukito and Prio Hartono full time; and Muhd Usman, Rusli Alif, Aminamza, and Rachman Pane part time. The office was Bapak's large garage.

Meantime Bapak was preparing to establish a Subud Centre and had begun looking for land south of Jakarta. He asked me to design a house for him. Although I protested that I was not an architect, he said 'It's all the same, engineer or architect.' He made a rough sketch of the floor plan from which I drew a house and made a balsawood model. Helena and I worked every day at Bapak's house, I at a drawing board and she helping with typing and proofreading.

Within a few weeks of our arrival Bapak bought land in the area known as Cilandak (old spelling Tjilandak) near Pasar Mede. Much later when the Subud International Centre was built on this land it became known as *Wisma Subud.* In those days the district was completely rural, much of it paddy fields, and was well beyond the built-up area of the southern suburb of Kebayoran. Once the land was purchased we travelled every Sunday with Bapak and his wife Ibu and others out to the land for a picnic, sitting on mats on the grass under the shady trees.

Now Bapak asked me to leave the work on his house and design a guesthouse with nine double bedrooms and a dining room suitable for foreign visitors. From my experience working on Bapak's house I had become familiar with the basic principles of tropical architecture—orientation, sun screening and cross-ventilation. I also had a generous attitude towards the provision of bathrooms.

The building was to be of brick and have a reinforced concrete frame. In a few weeks I completed the drawings necessary for City Council approval.

I then set to work to survey the land and prepare a contour plan marking all the fruit trees for protection during development. Brodjo and Sudarto helped with the measurement. In all this, although Bapak and those around him had an adequate standard of living, there was no luxury. I noticed that the money for Subud activities was managed very carefully and was often the topic of discussion with Usman and others. Personal assets, such as jewellery, were often sold by the family to fund a new activity or purchase. Everyone was a trader. This was probably true of the whole society, which was still suffering from inflation of the currency. The black market exchange rate for the US dollar was something like four times the official rate.

It was at this time that Bapak published the first issue of the *Pewarta Kejiwaan Subud* (The Subud Reporter) magazine. Money was short and paper difficult to get but Bapak said it was the right time and it should go ahead. It was typed and assembled by the secretariat. Brodjo designed the first cover. There were stories of strange experiences connected with its production. At the printing shop, the non-Subud typesetters were affected by the text and fell asleep over their work. This I was told was the effect of the spiritual content of Bapak's writing on people who were not opened. Certainly I got quite dizzy when I thought too much while trying to improve the English translation.

We were children in the spiritual life, protected by our naivete and Bapak's tolerance. Our presence in Bapak's secretariat every day and my work on the buildings for Cilandak may have had the value of accustoming the members of the secretariat to foreigners. They were able to see our fallibility as much as our Western capacity for independence and action. Later, Usman, Haryono and Rachman, in whose homes we stayed, as well as the members of the secretariat, were all to be exposed to Europeans in their work for Subud.

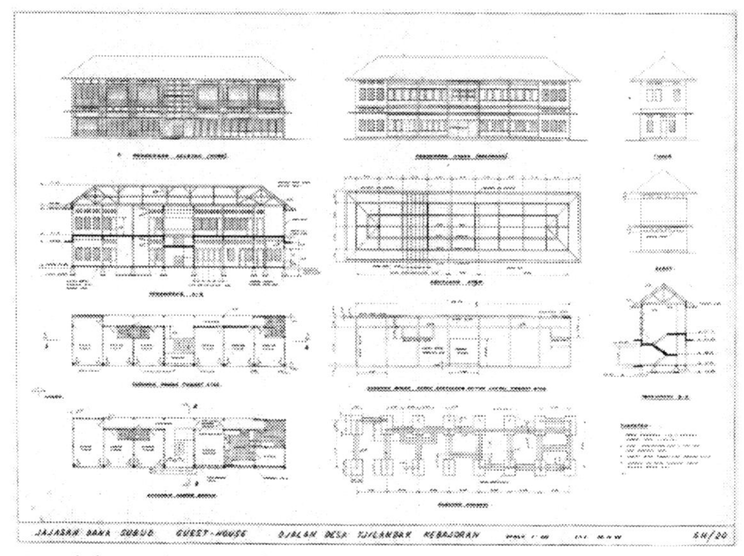

Detail design drawing of the Guesthouse, Cilandak, 25 October 1960

Hand sawing of timber on site for building components, Cilandak

2—*Subud World News, September 1973*

THE BROTHERHOOD OF SUBUD *continued*

by
MUHAMMAD RUSLI ALIF

In 1958 Bapak made a journey to several countries in Asia, and again visited England and some other countries in Europe. Then in 1959 Bapak presided at the First Subud World Congress, held at Coombe Springs, near London, after which he proceeded to other countries in Europe, and to America and Australia. All these tours were made while Bapak had his home in Jalan Djawa. On returning from the last trip, Bapak requested me to look for a site suitable for establishing guest houses and a latihan hall for foreign brothers and sisters who might wish to visit Indonesia, and for building a house there for Bapak. One of the three suggestions I made was the Cilandak site, which Bapak approved, and soon afterward the deal was closed. This was in 1960.

At that time, committee members and helpers used to sit with Bapak every Saturday night, the whole night through until morning, at Bapak's house at Jalan Djawa, listening to Bapak's various stories or kejiwaan experiences; and although we had been up all night, yet we felt fresh and healthy when leaving Bapak's house, and after having breakfast in our own homes, we later met Bapak again on the Cilandak site. The first foreign visitors we received before the Cilandak Complex was established were Keith Rogge from Holland, Viktor Gebers from South Africa, Elizabeth Aitken from New Zealand, Dr. Ruzo and his wife Ellya from Brazil, John Bennett and his wife Elizabeth from England, and Dr. Leonora Kuplis from Germany.

In August 1960 Bapak, as the Spiritual Guide of the Subud Brotherhood, started the International Secretariat Kejiwaan, consisting of S. Brodjolukito (who had previously acted as Bapak's secretary, replacing Indra Sjafrin who remained in England), Sudarto Martohudojo and Prio Hartono as full-time members, and Muhammad Usman, Muhammad Rusli Alif, Rachmad Pane and Aminamza as part-time members. From time to time, Dr. Achmad Subardjo Djojoadisurjo, the former Indonesian Foreign Minister and Ambassador, also gave assistance in translating the letters that began to flow in from abroad. Bapak also issued in that year the first official Subud magazine for the Subud World Brotherhood—the *Pewarta*. (From that beginning has developed a great deal of publishing activity connected with Bapak's talks and letters and writings, and this is now handled by Subud Publications International—S.P.I.—a sub-Committee of the main executive body of the Brotherhood: the International Subud Committee in Wolfsburg, Germany. To feed the S.P.I. with material, there has come into being at Cilandak a translating team of Indonesian and Western brothers and sisters, whose main task is to evolve an authoritative English text, from which translations into several other languages are also made. The best-known member of this team was the late Mariamah Wichmann. The translators, in turn, depend for their material on tape recordings transcribed into typed texts in the Secretariat).

Bapak also established in 1960 the first Subud company, with Mas Usman and myself as the managing directors, to which Bapak gave the name of *Karya Budhi Dharma*. This company, of which Bapak and his family are the main shareholders, started the construction of the first international guest house at Cilandak, in which Bapak stayed, after his house in Jalan Djawa had been sold and before his present home was built. Work on the Wisma Subud international complex was started by the Indonesian contractor Hadisaputro and our Australian brother Lamaan van Sommers, a civil engineer. (At various later times the Indonesian contractor Martono, and Subud architects Abdullah Pope, Ramzi Winkler and Lambert Gibbs, civil engineer Sjarif Horthy, and electrical engineer Irwan Maindonald all took part in its development.) The whole complex is administered by a foundation called *Yayasan Subud*.

The beginning of Cilandak and other Subud events 1958-1960

Bapak, Ibu and family at 68 Djalan Tjokroaminoto, Jakarta 1960

Usman, Arminah, family and friends at their house in Jakarta 1960

Bapak visiting the newly-purchased land at Cilandak in 1960

Bapak's secretariat in the garage of his house at 68 Djalan Tjokroaminoto, Jakarta, 1960. Left to right: Lionel & Helena van Sommers, Rachman Pane, Sudarto, Aminamza and Brodjolukito.

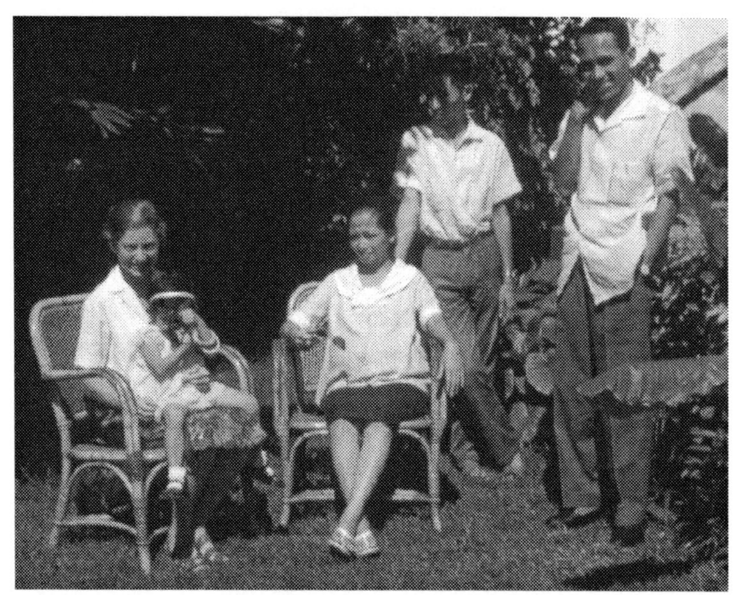

(left to right) Helena with Isti, Ismana, Ismana's brother, Haryono 1960

Picnic at the Temperate Climate Gardens, Cianjur, West Java 1960
(left to right) Haryono, Lionel and Helena, Isti, Rahayu, and Ismana

Bapak also used us an example to show the international character of Subud to other Indonesians. Officialdom under President Sukarno required that all religious movements be registered. Bapak sent me with Brodjo to the Department of Religion, where I was asked questions about Subud. Another time Bapak told an Islamic visitor that I said 'Allah' in my latihan. I had some doubt about this at the time, but in my next latihan I found myself repeating 'Allah, Allah' in a loud voice! I had no way of knowing if I had been influenced by Bapak's remark, but the exclamation continued from that time on to be a part of my latihan.

The atmosphere near Bapak was very much a family feeling and I felt close to those with whom we stayed. I enjoyed living in an ambience of feeling, so strong in Indonesian culture, rather than thinking. I was delighted with the sights, sounds and smells around me. I found the Indonesians I met were refined and sensitive and had that calm attentiveness which is the essence of good manners. Bapak treated us like everyone else with loving kindness and openness. We took part in most of the outings with him, going together to latihan, sitting talking about new developments in Subud, going on regular Sunday picnics to the land at Cilandak, and even attending an occasional local movie together.

We also joined Haryono and Ismana on many of their activities. Simple pleasures, like sitting out on the terrace in the cool of evening, listening to the hum of passing bicycle rickshaws and the sounds of vendors, and sharing coconut cakes cooked in steaming kettles by passing traders, were delights unmatched by any relaxation I had known in the West. We travelled with Haryono and his Dutch mining consultant, Mr Heyden, through bandit country to the gold mine at Cikotok in south-west Java. Together with Haryono, Ismana and Rahayu we went on outings to the mountains. We also became friends with Musa Djoemena, who had been Indonesian Ambassador to Portugal, and his family. Laughter was an important aspect of all relationships and the Indonesians I met had the capacity to enjoy life as it came without the need for luxuries.

I don't remember Bapak giving me any direct personal advice at that time, nor did he give general talks to members. We would sit in the secretariat while he discussed the day to day happenings. This was only translated on the rare occasion of a foreign visitor, or if one of the secretariat felt it was of particular interest to us (our Indonesian was still inadequate to understand). Among these translations, it was Bapak's seemingly casual remarks that I remember best. 'The latihan can be done any time, even after the movies,' he said. The emphasis from the translator was that the latihan can be done anytime, but the message that I got was quite different. It said to me, 'It is a good idea to do the latihan after the movies, or any other time that your feelings are invaded by an experience.' I came to realise that this way of passing on guidance was not only totally without pressure to learn (as from a teacher) but also it could by-pass the thinking and enter the inner feeling.

In August 1960, in order to extend our stay in Indonesia, we flew to Singapore to have our tourist visas replaced with short visit visas. We were put up in the flat next door to the NG Nair family at the Subud House at 18 Leicester Road for the two-week wait. During this time we went with Gordon (later Edward) van Hien and Maarten Giel to Kota Baru in Kelantan, on the north east coast of Malaysia, to open a group of local people who had been gathered together by Arifin, a local Malaysian member. We travelled the thousand kilometre round trip in two cars, crossing fourteen river ferries and staying in Government rest houses on the beaches. We arrived to find a crowd of candidates collected at a small sportsground pavilion. For several hours we opened group after group—more than seventy men in one weekend. Until that time I had opened few people and it was evidence of the miracle of the latihan to see the spontaneous movement and song of these brothers. While I was there, I opened the older brother of the Sultan of Kelantan in the privacy of his palace. Later Bapak recounted this story of the Christians opening the Muslims.

On our return to Jakarta Usman had completed an extension to his house and we were invited to stay with him, relieving the pressure for space on Haryono and Ismana. We stayed with Usman and Aminah for about three months and then moved again to live with Rachman Pane and his mother, nearer to Bapak's house.

More and more I loved Indonesia and the Indonesian people. As the latihan enlivened my feelings, I delighted in the simple daily impressions. I wrote at the time:

'Rachman lives in the residential district of Menteng in a main street lined with fine old Dutch houses. Some have been converted for business use. Although it is a good class neighbourhood, behind the elegant plastered bungalows, and clustered along the steep banks of a yellow-brown stream, there is a small slum village of bamboo shacks. This afternoon I stood there, resting one foot on the bridge railing, looking down into the river. It was a clear hot day and a light breeze was cooling the humid air. I could see the shacks jumbled together above the high water mark and separated from the water by a pile of rubbish and a few banana trees. Peals of laughter were coming from the children jumping into the water from the rafts of bamboo moored in the stream. A mother on a raft was soaping and bathing a small brown body. Simple coloured kites in red and white, on strings that reached just above the trees, soared and dived as they were tugged and released to catch the wind. I felt myself part of what I was watching—and yet separate—the bridge, the stream, the shacks, the rubbish, the children, and the kites.'

Now with barely enough funds to get started, Usman arranged for a building contractor to begin construction of the guesthouse. It was to be a race to get the foundations complete before the monsoon rains. I began to go to the site to check the work and answer any questions. I remember travelling out one day with a member, Rolandin. He said to me, 'Since my crisis* my tongue can taste the harmony or disharmony that has occurred during the building of a house. It is very important that all of you who work on the Subud guesthouse are in harmony so that the people who come later and live in it will have a good feeling.' I believed him, never imagining it would be otherwise.

* A rapid acceleration of the spiritual process of the latihan.

Bapak visiting the Cilandak land with family members in 1961
(left to right) Bapak's mother, Tuti, Adji and Hardiyati

Rice paddy-fields immediately behind the Cilandak land 1961

Hardly had this idea been registered in my mental list of good intentions than I had a disagreement with the Indonesian contractor when he wanted to reduce the amount of steel reinforcement in the foundations. I had been on the safe side when I calculated the steel but being young and inexperienced did not have the flexibility to reconsider my specification. Our argument came to Bapak's attention and, although he didn't say anything, I understood through Usman that it would be better if I were to leave the contractor to do the work his own way. 'There is no place for the generosity of materials that is normal in the West,' Usman said. 'Here every bag of cement has to be bartered for and every reinforcing bar is expensive.'

Bapak did not want to go ahead with his own house, so, with no other work to be done, I asked him if we should now go on to New Zealand, as he had earlier advised us to do in England. He agreed. We had been in Jakarta for six months. Before we left Indonesia we arranged to visit Yogyakarta, the ancient capital of Java. We contacted the Subud group, some of whom were longtime members from the days when Bapak lived there. They were exceedingly kind to us, taking us at a leisurely pace by horse and carriage to see the tourist sights. The main attraction was the world-famous Borobudur Buddhist stupa built in AD 778-850. On the way we visited the large complex of Hindu temples of Prambanan, of a later period, located on the Yogyakarta plain. I was feeling very sensitive, noticing the difference of atmosphere in the many shrines, and when I came to Borobudur I clearly felt that I wanted to be alone. I began walking around the stone terraces, winding my way up the seven levels of the unique open air temple. The walls of the lower four levels were carved with elaborate scenes illustrating man's outer life, while at intervals on all four sides were statues of seated Bodhisattvas in cave-like recesses. The three upper terraces were circular with plain walls, two with rings of perforated stone bell-shaped retreats containing larger-than-life seated Buddha figures in meditation. Finally the pyramid was topped with a huge single solid bell-shaped centrepiece. Here, as I paused before it, wondering at its meaning, I passed into a state of bliss, then into an ecstasy of transcendent oneness. ... As I came out of it I knew that this was the experience intended by the builders of the stupa.

On 18 January 1961 we took the ship *Willem Ruys* from Jakarta to Melbourne. We visited our families and began to adjust back into a Western culture. It was not always easy. After being entirely with Bapak and Subud members for six months, I now on occasions felt physically nauseated and distressed when I was with non-Subud people. I was sensitive to the forces but still did not know how inwardly to separate from my responses. On 19 April we re-boarded the same ship and sailed to New Zealand.

I now turned my attention to finding a job in consulting engineering. In England I had been part of a team of engineers investigating the application of prestressed concrete, a relatively new technique in tensioned steel reinforcement, and had studied the design methods of the American Professor T.Y. Lyn, a world leader at the time. In New Zealand, on the strength of my short experience, I applied for and got the job of design engineer for a company in Tauranga producing prestressed concrete bridges. It transpired that this technique suited the economy of New Zealand and my interest in its application had started me on a successful career. This 'happy coincidence' I would later see as guidance.

Within a year, as a result of my Tauranga experience, I was offered the position of Resident Engineer for a new Arts and Library building for Victoria University in Wellington. The job was practical project management, the type of work that Bapak had confirmed as my right work back in 1957 in Coombe Springs. Over the next three years I supervised the construction of a ten-storey high-rise building made up of precast concrete parts, prestressed together. It was the first of its kind in New Zealand and won awards for its innovative design. At the same time, negotiating and managing the financial and quality aspects of the contract brought me daily in contact with strong-willed building contractors, an experience which helped me quickly become a more self-reliant engineer. When the building was completed I was appointed manager of the Wellington office responsible for supervising the construction of a computer centre for the Bank of New Zealand.

University Arts and Library Building, Wellington, NZ 1962-64

Innovative prestressed concrete construction in an active earthquake zone

New Zealand Subud members 1963. On the left Irwan Maindonald who later established PT Asian Area Consultants in Jakarta.

Victoria University Wellington, library interior 1965

Meantime in Subud we had a congress in Christchurch and I found myself elected National Chairman of Subud New Zealand, with the particular task of producing a constitution and arranging incorporation. In March 1963 Bapak visited New Zealand and came to Wellington. Not having our own hall, we hired the Friends House for the latihans. As Bapak entered the building he paused and said, 'These people [Quakers] had something real in the beginning.' [When their movement started.]

On the following nights Bapak gave three talks at the house of Dorita Edmunson in the room where the group usually held latihans. In the final talk he gave this guidance:

Brothers and sisters, Bapak would like to explain about the desires, which are in fact the obstacles in your worship of Almighty God. There are four kinds of desires. The first is called angkara, the second murka, the third keinginan, and the fourth jatmika. The influence of angkara in your inner feeling causes you to want to sow dissension, to quarrel, to argue; in short, to create a commotion or disturbance. The second is murka. If it influences your inner feeling, it causes you to want to be the best, to want to win, to want to be the cleverest. In short, you do not like to be surpassed, you do not like to be exceeded or even equalled by other people. And keinginan is the desire that causes you to want to possess things that you have seen and thought about.

The fourth is jatmika, the desire that is gentle, that likes to give way and to help: to help one's fellow human beings, to show love and affection towards others, and to be in harmony. The fourth desire is the desire that can always accept, so it causes a person to remember to worship God and to remember their responsibility as a human being who has been given life by the power of God.

Indeed, these four kinds of desire are necessary for human beings, so that they may possess enthusiasm, the motivation to go after what they need; because without these desires people would have no enthusiasm to work. But human beings should be careful; they need to reflect that their desires —which create the enthusiasm that motivates their wish to know something or possess something, or whatever—need to be limited.

And as for how to limit these desires, for this we need to use the fourth desire: to ensure that we do not use the other desires excessively.

However, at the times when you worship God you do not need to use the desires. You should not let them have any power or influence over your inner feeling; because when the desires are there, God cannot give you anything, and you yourself cannot possibly receive what you ought to receive. ... [Recording 63 WLG 3]

At the end of one talk Bapak did testing. He asked me to show: 'How does a racehorse feel when it is being ridden in a race?' My response was immediate. I felt the experience of the racehorse and galloped spontaneously with tremendous exhilaration. (To the laughter of everyone!)

This was the first time I had been personally tested by Bapak and the experience made a very strong impression on me. Although the horse was being used by the rider, I felt its nature was to respond automatically and gallop. It was a long time before I understood that this test was intended to show me that I had the propensity to be used by others and yet at the same time to feel good about it, even exhilarated.

He had earlier explained that testing was carried out by simply doing the latihan after asking a question:

In order to be able to receive and to feel a test, you are not required to do anything but to remain in the state of receiving your latihan; that is, not to think and imagine things, not to identify with anything, not to represent any picture for yourself, but only receive as in the latihan. Testing in its nature is similar to following the latihan.

The years in Wellington were very pleasant. The work was interesting and we had good friends in the Subud group. We lived well, renting a comfortable house with a wide view of the harbour. We visited and entertained, we gardened and kept bees. During this time I heard news of the political unrest in Indonesia, first the confrontation with Malaysia and then the serious internal struggle for power that culminated in the deposing of President Sukarno and the banning of the Communist party, however I felt myself settled in New Zealand and didn't relate personally to these events.

In mid-1966 an unexpected series of events took place which was to change all that. It started when Helena's sister suggested that we might take care of her new baby, with a view to adoption. We wanted to start a family but we were undecided about the idea of adoption. At this point I saw, in the latihan, a house in the area for sale. I took it as an indication to accept the offer to take care of the baby. I located the house and we bought it. Soon afterwards the mother decided that she didn't want to part with her child. We were happy with the house purchase and I concluded that it had nothing to do with the possibility of adopting the baby. The mother had simply changed her mind.

At this point Ramzi Winkler and Tom (Abdullah) Pope wrote to say that Bapak had suggested they set up an architects' and engineers' consulting company in Jakarta and that I come back as engineer. The proposal was that we would provide the design services for the continuing development of the Subud complex in Cilandak and at the same time develop a commercial enterprise for projects outside. I liked the idea of returning to Indonesia to take part in Bapak's activities again, but found that I could not sell the house for enough to repay the mortgage, without first renovating. As that would take some weeks, we decided to go to Indonesia. I would return later to work on the house. We sold all our personal belongings, including part of Helena's jewellery (a sacrifice which, in retrospect, I should not have expected) and raised enough money to buy our air tickets. We arrived in Cilandak on 21 November 1966. It was my thirty-eighth birthday.

Ramzi, Abdullah and I immediately started work. Bapak gave us a space in the front of the old latihan hall, near the secretariat. We had to take any job we could get and began with the remodelling of the Australian Ambassador's house in Menteng. Abdullah made the contact, Ramzi prepared the detail drawings and I managed the contracts and services. At the same time I turned my attention to an apartment building for Erling Week and Abdullah in Wisma Subud which was being built without engineering supervision and where parts of the concrete structure were in danger of collapse.

Although our work outside Wisma Subud was not for Bapak I felt that everything we were doing was for his mission and under his guidance. This was dramatically illustrated for me in February 1967 when Bapak departed on a world tour. I went back to New Zealand to prepare my house for sale. I was doing all the renovation work myself and it was going slowly when one night in mid-May I had a vivid and impacting dream. I saw Bapak coming back to Wisma Subud from the World Congress in Japan and with him about a hundred people. In the dream Bapak told me that he needed another floor on the guesthouse to accommodate these visitors. I awoke filled with a great sense of urgency—I had to get back to Indonesia and put that extra floor on the guesthouse. There was also pressure for me to finish the house so I could settle my affairs finally in New Zealand. I don't know where the energy came from, but I worked day and night for the next seven days, barely sleeping. I was able to mobilise Subud friends and together we completed new plumbing, wiring and painting. The amazing thing was the amount of work we were able to do. In the last few hours I packed all my household belongings and organised the sale of the house through a friend as we drove together to the plane. I arrived in Cilandak in a heightened state of consciousness and immediately organised the extra floor of the guesthouse. Repeating the floor below was straightforward concrete construction, but the underground drainage system built in 1961 had to be completely rebuilt. When construction got under way and the structure was loaded with tonnes of concrete and masonry, the question arose in my mind, *had the contractor put sufficient reinforcement steel in the foundations back in 1960!* It seems that he had, because the building neither settled nor cracked. The work was finished just in time for Bapak's return in August when he was followed by a hundred people who needed accommodation, as the dream had shown.

~

Cilandak guesthouse after the third floor was added in 1967

Visitors meeting on the guesthouse porch in the early 1970s

Chapter Six

Subud in Indonesia

In November 1966 Indonesia was still recovering from the trauma of the 1965 coup by the Army and the massive purge that had followed. The tension which existed under Sukarno and the Communists had gone, but local security was still a concern. In Wisma Subud there was a night guard to patrol the compound. Bapak would sit up with the men every night until after midnight, usually outside the secretariat. He would then go to his office and work until 2 am. The rostered two-man guard would stay awake until dawn.

At these sittings, which were attended by up to a dozen men, Bapak would quietly let the conversation develop, talking about everyday things. Sometimes he answered questions. Although there was some practical need for the security of a night guard, it was well understood that the content of these gatherings was the inner experience. Reducing sleep was a common *prehatin* (self denial) practised in Indonesia to subdue the *nafsu* (passions) and, although Bapak was not teaching us with words, he was using these occasions to give spiritual help. He left it to us to respect this and to stay inwardly aware. This routine continued every night for about two years.

It didn't occur to me at the time, but there was a certain ambiguity in my attitude in going back to Indonesia. Subud—following the latihan—did not require the help of a teacher or guru, and yet my principal motive in going back to Indonesia was to be near Bapak.

Bapak's mother Eyang with Istimah Week's mother Mayko 1967

Bapak talking with men outside the latihan hall, Cilandak 1967

Bapak, Ibu and Arminah departing from Jakarta for the 1967 World Tour

Members gathering at the entrance to the old latihan hall 1967

Bapak was of course father to everyone. Every aspect of life in Wisma Subud was lived within the ambience of his values and guidance. We were members of his extended family, gradually acquiring his outlook and his customs. Bapak took an interest in everything that happened, he attended countless latihans, gave hundreds of talks and testing, directed the affairs of the community and initiated new projects. He also gave personal advice, directly when requested and spontaneously when the occasion arose.

Luckily he was the ideal father, because he was not only a reliable and loving protector, strong and wise, but he also encouraged his children to find their own independence and maturity. This enabled us to be in the community and yet strive to be somebody apart.

Although the political situation in Indonesia in 1966 was stable, the economic condition was still depressed. This meant that Bapak depended on money coming from overseas. The advantage of this was that the cost of building, such as Bapak's house, with local materials and local labour, was extremely low in US dollars terms. Against this Bapak saw the opportunity to press ahead with the development of Cilandak and other projects putting a high demand on the available funds. Usman, as financial manager for Bapak, had the task of deciding the priorities. Running expenses often competed with new development costs, and funds were co-mingled. Usman had to be pragmatic to meet Bapak's goals.

Living in Cilandak I did a lot of latihan. For a while it was a vicious circle. The more latihans I did, the more I felt I needed to do. The whole thing was a kind of *crisis*—doing more latihan, following Ramadhan to extreme by staying up all night, doing Monday and Thursday fasting, and adding any other form of self-denial that I could find. It was a purification of the self-will—I was trying to measure up to standards that I set for myself. It ran its course for two years then gradually the self-will lost its force. I began to see that the need was not 'to try to remember the latihan at all times' (an act of will which was impossible) but to 'not forget the latihan.' This change of centre from my self-will to my inner guidance (attitude) brought me enormous relief and better results.

Bapak's house designed by Ramzi Winkler

Meantime there were special moments when Bapak saw the opportunity and gave some personal guidance.

I found Bapak's personal advice, however informal the tone, or minor the occasion, was always important. When he helped me, he dealt with fundamental obstacles in my spiritual life. For example, one of the earliest happenings I remember during this time was at the completion of his house. I felt I'd like to give Ibu (Bapak's wife) a present for the occasion. I had little money, but I asked Bapak what Ibu would like. Shortly afterwards he called me and said, 'Come, we'll go to Pasar Baru.' This was a Jakarta street with shops that sold Indonesian paintings, carvings, ornaments, and so on. Usman, who was driving, parked the car and led the way along the crowded pavement to a shop that had silver figurines made in Yogyakarta. Bapak looked at them with interest and said, 'I think Ibu would like that betjak (bicycle rickshaw).' I thought it was nice and was delighted that Bapak seemed pleased. Bapak went on looking and said, 'Yes, this one of the woman sitting at the loom, I'm sure Ibu would like that one too.' 'Yes, er ...' I said, somewhat surprised. Bapak went on looking and pointed to a figure of a street trader and my solar plexus started to tighten. At that point Bapak brought me face to face with the power of the material force in myself. He was quiet for a while longer and then said, 'Ya, ya.' (Meaning 'that'll do'.)

At first I thought *Bapak had shown me that the measure of giving is how much it hurts,* but later I realised that he had taken me though a barrier in my character so that I could recognise and know how to handle the material force.

Bapak also helped in other ways—direct ways beyond the heart and mind. One day on a Sunday outing to his farm at Patjet, Bapak was sitting talking with us on the terrace. We were about a dozen men. The ladies were inside with Ibu. When Bapak talked I always relaxed and felt the latihan, so my mind would quieten. This was so normal that I can't say I noticed anything different that day. But at a certain moment Bapak looked at me and started to talk.

I felt so open that his words passed into me without obstruction and went on into some place deep inside me. I felt like an open window through which Bapak was speaking. He was talking to my inner self. I just stayed perfectly still, in that receptive state, as Bapak continued to talk for half an hour or more.

Suddenly I wavered ever so slightly. Bapak stopped and it was over. I had followed the feeling of what he was saying rather than the detail and could not remember what he said. The nearest I can say was that he was talking to my past, or to that part of my soul that had been in the past. But I felt changed. I felt more connected with my past, more connected with my ancestry.

In those early days in Cilandak I would occasionally visit Sudarto at his home in the evening and ask his interpretation of a dream*. The things he said about dreams were mostly explanations of the symbolism rather than interpretations of the personal meaning. He was always hospitable and kindly. Sometimes we would be alone, at other times with a few others who had come to ask questions or simply listen to his spiritual experiences. He often volunteered his advice on how we should benefit from being near Bapak. When I started to go to his house in December 1966 I made notes of what Sudarto said:

'When Bapak talks with us late into the night he gradually raises the spiritual level. By so doing one by one those present fall asleep. He then drops the level and each one wakes up. What Bapak talks about may be daily matters, but at the same time Bapak is passing things to our inner feeling, individually. If we are sensitive we will feel this happen.

'If we use our thinking when we are with Bapak (on these nights) we will also probably fall asleep. A useful technique for freeing oneself from thinking is to drop the tongue from of the palate and breathe easily —if possible receiving the latihan at the same time.

* Bapak's explanation about dreams at the Tokyo Congress in 1967 was that whereas most dreams are a projection of a person's own unresolved concerns, there are 'sometimes, too, dreams which are an indication of what is going to happen.'

'If we are ten per cent purified then we are taken care of by our guidance ten per cent, the remaining ninety per cent has to be dealt with by the passions. Sometimes Bapak may see that a purification will take a long time but he doesn't tell the member because it would only cause the person to feel discouraged. Instead Bapak indicates the direction and improvement possible bit by bit—like when one wants a child to cross the room one offers a series of attractions which will encourage the child across.

'While undergoing purification it is better to find a job which you really understand and which satisfies your feelings.'

Sudarto often spoke at that time about the reported signs of Bapak's coming and what Bapak would bring:

Rofé, he said, found in Holland a prophesy written five hundred years ago, that said a man bringing a true message would be born at the same time as three kings. Bapak was born in the same month as Sukarno, and the same year as Leopold III and Emperor Hirohito.

Bapak's great grandfather had a vision before he died that his third generation descendant would receive the way to God. This was passed down to Bapak's parents. Bapak's mother experienced a light from heaven entering her and radiating from her body during her pregnancy.

Sudarto also liked to advise the visitors about their relationship with women:

'A woman's nature is of this world—of the heart—so if her heart is satisfied then she is satisfied. A woman likes her man to be relaxed so that the vibration from his inner feeling will enter her heart and she will be satisfied. Every woman has an affinity for a certain flower. If we see this flower in our latihan, [it is a sign that] our wife will love us.'

I enjoyed the company of my Indonesian brothers. I often visited Haryono and would go out to eat with him and Asikin and sometimes Sjafrudin (Bapak's son-in-law). Such occasions were full of fun. Talking was always mixed with laughing and joking.

In 1967 Sjafrudin died. I happened to be near him at the time and at Ibu's request I tried to revive him, giving mouth to mouth resuscitation. He showed no signs of life and I soon felt I should stop. His death was a great shock. He was only thirty-five years old but had had a heart attack. He left a young wife and four children.

The Subud Indonesia National Congress was held in Cilandak immediately after the 1967 World Congress in Toyko. It was attended by more than a hundred foreign visitors— Americans, English, French and Germans—and a hundred and fifty Indonesians from other centres. With the local members we were about four hundred. The guesthouse kitchen was extended and a large round bamboo building was erected as a dining hall. People flowed out on to the lawns and gathered, often in national groups, chatting under the trees. The atmosphere was like a festival.

For those of us who were unable to go to Japan the National Congress offered the opportunity to hear Bapak's assessment of the World Congress proceedings and then to share his talks to the local delegates. Bapak said that in Japan the number of days devoted to discussion and debate was reduced significantly by 'finding solutions which are at the point of balance between everything to the right and left.' This was only possible, he said, by the Grace of God. Where his talks in Japan covered primary topics such as the principles of Subud, its origins and growth, and the development of Cilandak, his three talks to the Indonesia Congress were addressed to the personal needs of members, with detailed explanations of how the lower life forces influence human lives, the need to work, and how our actions can be assessed. This is an excerpt from Bapak's first talk on August 20:

Brothers and sisters, it is very necessary for you to be very careful and vigilant in all your actions. And in order to be vigilant you need to be free from self-interest and be based on the feeling of patience, submission and sincerity. ... Based on patience, submission and sincerity, your inner feeling will become free from the influence of the nafsu and then you will be able to feel how the life forces work within your self.

In the inner feeling you will be able to regulate the connection of the material life force that is within you with the material life force that is outside you. ... Thus you have to remember that these various forces are within you. What are they ? They are created within you as servants. This is the Will of God. For if these various forces, the forces of raiwani *(material),* nabadi *(vegetable),* chewani *(animal) and* djasmani *(human) were not within you, you would just remain like a statue. Yes. For that which is able to look for money is the force of* raiwani, *brothers and sisters. If there is no satanic (material) force in you, you cannot find money. Do not abandon Satan. No! That will get you into trouble. If you are left by Satan, then in ten days you will have no money. What is important for you is the way you make use of the satanic force. Use the material force when you look for money. Use the vegetable force when you plant this or plant that. Use the animal force when you eat meat. Also, use the* djasmani *force when you marry and when you come together with your wife. Thus, these forces are very necessary for your life because with them present you become a complete being, a perfect being, called* Insan kamil *[a perfect human being].*

To convince you about the result of any action you undertake, it is written in the holy books, the Psalms, the Old Testament, the New Testament and the Qur'an, and it is also said in the sayings of people who lived long ago who received Grace from Almighty God, that before taking an action you should first check it with the following: Dzat *(the Essence),* Sifat *(the Fact, the Nature),* Asma *(the Application, the Practice),* Afngal *(the Result). You need to take these four factors into consideration.* Dzat *means* kersa *(will that comes from the inner feeling). But your will is called* karep*—that is, imagination, picturing of ideas, intellect. For example: first you have the idea of becoming a doctor. Then you really become a doctor , that is the* sifat *of it, the fact.* Asma *means to practise; after you have become a doctor you should practise what you have learned and prove whether or not you can cure somebody who is suffering—for instance, from an ulcer. Just an ulcer, first; do not go deeper than that as yet. If your prescription is effective and you can really do the job as a doctor, then you can be called doctor. Thus, the* afgnal, *the result, has become a reality.*

So do not just stay doing nothing, saying 'Bismillahir rochmanir rachim, qul huallahhu ahad' *[Islamic prayer: 'In the name of God the Compassionate, the Merciful. Say He is the One and Only God.'] and with this expect money to fall into your lap. Don't do that. God will not give you money if you do not work, because there is no money in heaven. Up there is no money as it is made here. So do not just daydream or do* samadi *(meditation) or just pray in order to receive money, no. You have to work! We have already experienced this fact, brothers and sisters, through the latihan kedjiwaan. The latihan, in fact, brings to life all our five senses; all our physical organs come to life. If all these are alive, it is an indication that we must work.* [Recording 67 TJK 5]

In his last talk Bapak elaborated on the effect of the each of the lower forces in our lives with many examples from Javanese stories and myths. Then at the close of the Congress there was an all-night *wayang* performance (shadow-puppet show). Although wayang shows were still common throughout Indonesia, we seldom had an opportunity to see a classical performance and moreover by a top *dalang* (puppet master). The music was provided by a full gamelan orchestra of about a dozen instruments—gambangs (wooden and metal xylophones), gongs, drums and stringed instruments—with the players sitting in front of the white screen. The dalang with his hundreds of flat leather puppets sat behind, so that we in the audience saw only the shadows of the intricately-designed and stylised puppets as they moved, quivering and tilting. The dalang, accompanied by the high treble voice of the female singer, spoke the voices of heroes and villains of an episode from the great Mahabharata myth. Although I had no idea of the story, the sound conveyed the drama. The tension waxed and waned, high points emphasised by the percussion, serenity created by long phrases from the soprano, and humour in its turn from the versatile voice of the dalang. As dawn approached and the climax of the story broke upon us with a crescendo of sound, I swear the flickering light behind the screen turned to fire. The battle between good and evil was over. The gods from the safety of heaven sang their haunting song of reconciliation.

Like others who had come to live in Cilandak I was concerned with my inner life, with the effects on my feelings of things happening inside and out. Bapak's talks gave direction to the development of my understanding. His explanations were timely and were based on the experiences we all shared. For example, at the end of Ramadhan he talked about how we felt and how we handled the results of fasting; in other talks he explained what we were experiencing in our relationships, and proposed solutions to our concerns; and on his birthday, when guests performed dances and sang, he explained to us about culture.

When Bapak gave a talk I would come out moved by the wisdom of what he had said, then two days later I could recall very little. However, as time went on I found that certain things had remained and had become part of my understanding. For example about culture:

'Kebudayaan' *(culture) means in Indonesian: 'Actions through receiving from God.' True culture is expressed through dancing and singing when the parts of the body are already clean and God's power can flow through them.*

If we can follow this we should then be careful not to take as our own what we receive from God. Next to heaven is hell and the higher we rise also the greater the fall if we make a mistake. This is the reason that in Islam every action is prefaced with the prayer: Bismillahi-r-Rahmani-r-Rahim.*' ('In the name of Allah, the Beneficent, the Merciful.')*

In those days I often dropped into the secretariat for an hour or so to sit and enjoy the peaceful company. Sometimes Bapak would be there and I would listen to him discussing things. If Bapak sensed I needed to know something he might involve me in the conversation. At other times if Bapak was not there, Sudarto might volunteer to speak about something that had come up in the correspondence or that he felt was important to share. About the working of Bapak's secretariat he said that Bapak replied to most spiritual questions and was the only one who answered questions about fate: names, partners, occupations, and places to live.

He said that he himself helped with some spiritual questions, 'not because of a high soul, but because of wide and long experience.' Brodjo, he said, helped Bapak with general matters and Prio with matters of organisation. Usman was responsible for finance.

Indonesia was a predominantly Islamic country and the effect of this religious environment was that a number of Subud members were converted to Islam. Although I was not active in my Christian religion neither was I attracted to join Islam just because others were doing so. I respected the teaching of Islam and was aware of its place in the religious history of the West. I also noticed that Moslems in Indonesia had a greater sense of brotherhood than Christians in my own society. In October 1968 I had a clear dream:

I was dressed in a simple long white linen robe walking alone down a road in open countryside. I came to a place where the road divided into two and as I arrived I heard my name called from the minaret of a mosque down the left hand fork.

I awoke with the feeling that I would like to enter Islam.

Soon afterwards, together with six other Westerners, I went through the preparations and on 30 October 1968 before about two hundred guests made the declaration of faith: 'There is no God but the One God, and Muhammad is God's Messenger.'

At this ceremony Bapak gave me the Islamic name *Lamaan*.

This conversion had a strong impact on me. I felt cleansed by the circumcision. I learned the five daily prayers and practised them conscientiously. I felt that I was starting a new inner life. I accepted the value of the annual Ramadhan fast observed by the majority of Subud members in Indonesia and committed to it, otherwise conversion was a very personal experience and therefore remained a private matter. I never identified with the wider public aspect of membership of Islam such as worshipping in a mosque or seriously studying the teachings of the Koran.

Helena also joined and was given the name *Hassanah*.

In the months that followed I attended the general latihan held three times a week in the hall near Bapak's house in Cilandak and the extra latihans for men helpers with Bapak. In one of these latihans for helpers I had a strong spiritual experience. As I stood with my eyes closed a bright light came towards me and entered me. I felt that it came from a high source. It filled my body so that for a few moments I was completely made of light. My whole body was transparent light. I was conscious within it and outside it and in all directions. It was a wonderful experience and the knowledge of it has never left me.

In those times we saw Bapak every day. He would come to the secretariat during working hours, and regularly sit with the men on someone's porch in the evenings. We would also go with him when he went up to the hills on a Sunday. On one of these trips I was sitting out with some visitors on the terrace. Bapak began to explain that when we have the latihan alive in us we can understand things through any part of our body. For example, he said, 'Bapak's hand can read Lamaan's way of doing things.' He then proceeded to let his hand move: up for a while, then across for a while, up again for a while, then across again. This way of acting: action, stand back, action, stand back, he said, was in my character. 'This means,' he said, 'that Lamaan starts something, then leaves it for a while and then goes on with it.'

I was unaware of this characteristic and it was some time before I noticed the truth of it. Some years later a secretary told me that I had this pattern of behaviour. She did not know what Bapak had said to me.

My health was always good in Indonesia but at one stage I began to get chronic hay fever. Melbourne was a bad place for this and my mother suffered severely in the pollen season. I thought my attack may have been caused by some kind of spiritual stress or purification, rather than pollen. I went to see Bapak and told him my problem. He simply laughed. The hay fever stopped and never returned.

As the Wisma Subud community grew in numbers so did the social life. There were many selamatans, a kind of thanksgiving party for all occasions—birthdays, circumcisions, and new names—and at intervals of 3, 10, 40, 100 and 1000 days after someone died. As we were living in a bed-sitting room in the guesthouse, it suited us to spend most evenings out after dinner. My first choice was to go to where ever Bapak was sitting, outside the secretariat or on Usman's front porch. Women visited each other indoors. Overseas visitors liked to go to the homes of Mas Sudarto and Prio Hartono where they could ask questions and listen to stories. I also continued to visit those I had known in 1960—Haryono and Ismana, Asikin, and Usman and Aminah—and for a time we played tennis in the late afternoon. This was the outer activity of an inner life aspiring to human values, and it made community life an experience beyond any other I had ever known. It was a taste of a Golden Age.

In early 1968 Hassanah and I went with Rahayu to stay two weeks with Eyang, Bapak's mother, in Semarang. This was the house in Bergota Kalisari where Bapak received the latihan. Bapak's mother (Ibu Kursinah) was eighty three at the time. She stood very erect and appeared in good health. She had a quiet dignity and a gentle loving manner that made her entirely endearing. As well as Rahayu coming regularly from Jakarta, part of Eyang's extended family from Yogyakarta visited and lived with her. She was active, going to the market, enjoying cooking, and delighting in the babies of her grandchildren.

We shared in the daily activities of the household, going to visit members of the family and out to entertainments such as the Wayang Orang—the Wayang plays presented by actors instead of puppets. We met Bapak's younger sister, a very active and intelligent person, who with her husband ran a highly-respected clinic and pharmacy in the area. I became very fond of Rahayu and Eyang. When we returned to Jakarta we regularly visited Rahayu and her husband Pak Menggung at their house in Menteng.

Bapak's mother Eyang, Hassanah and Rahayu, Semarang 1968

Bapak's house, Semarang 1968

During our visit to Semarang we visited Pak Slamet and had latihan at his house. (He was one of the first two or three people to receive the latihan from Bapak). The room where we did the latihan was so small that only four or five of us could fit at one time. The remainder sat quietly outside and waited, one going in as one came out. This meant that much of the evening was spent waiting for the half-hour latihan, but this was the normal tempo of life in central Java and it was quite usual for people to sit up late into the night.

Pak Slamet was an artist, respected for his paintings of the spiritual character of people. I commissioned a painting which he later brought to Jakarta. It was a large Javanese landscape in vivid tropical colours showing a figure in a forest in the mountains. What I found interesting was his explanation that the forest, as a place where certain animals feel safe, symbolised my capacity to provide a secure environment for certain technically-qualified people—in the sense of providing work for their skill—was pertinent to my role as employer in IDC.

Much of Javanese culture was concerned with the inner life. However these interests were not all directed towards the worship of God, as in Subud. Magic and the use of spiritual forces to achieve one's aims were not uncommon. I found that even among some Indonesian Subud members interest in magic was not far away.

On one occasion a member from central Java, who saw that we did not have children, offered to lend me a kris—a magical dagger. He said I should put it under my pillow at night. I could not offend him so I accepted the dagger. Then I went to see Sudarto and told him the story. I said that I didn't want to get mixed up in magic. 'Oh, that's very easy,' he said, 'You put the kris away in a safe place, say at the office, and wait for about two weeks. Then you return the kris to its owner and tell him that you had a very big experience. You say that you put the dagger under your pillow and as a result you had the most extraordinary dream. He will be most interested, but you then have to say that in the dream you were told that you were not to tell anyone, not even him.'

I did as Sudarto said, and sure enough my helpful friend was completely satisfied.

Even senior public figures in Indonesia had their *dukuns* (soothsayers) and owned magical objects. There was a story at the time that General Suharto had been advised by his dukun that he should obtain the mask of Gadjah Madah if he was to have the confidence to confront President Sukarno. The mask was said to be endowed with the wisdom and power of Gadjah Madah, the Javanese warrior/ prime minister of the Madjapahit Empire—1295-1525. The story was that General Suharto went to great lengths to obtain a loan of this magical mask from Bali and as a result his confidence increased to the point where he could finally take over the role of President. Such stories were of great interest to the Javanese.

In October 1969 I travelled to Australia for two weeks with Haryono and Ismana and Istimah Week visiting the Melbourne and Sydney groups as helpers. This was one of Haryono's first trips abroad for Subud and he was well received, bringing a light touch to difficult problems.

In December 1969 Bapak and his family made a two-week journey around Java. This was immediately following the Ramadhan fast when according to custom Indonesians visit their elders. I went along and kept a diary:

Saturday 27 December 1969

CILANDAK. Today was the eighteenth birthday of Muti, Bapak's granddaughter, and this evening Ibu arranged a party in the Big House for Bapak's family and the residents. It was a quiet affair, partly because the lights had failed and the sitting room was lit only with pressure lamps. It finished at 10 pm so Bapak can make an early start tomorrow on a trip to East Java. The family has invited us and others to go.

At the start of Bapak's trip around Java 1969. Right: Erling Week

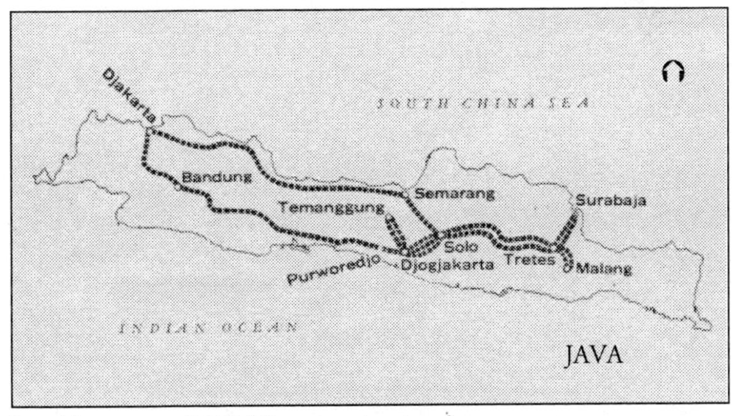

Bapak's route … 2,500 kilometres in nine days

Sunday 28 December 1969

SEMARANG. Indonesians joke about their disregard for time—djam karet (rubber time) they call it—but not Bapak. This morning he was as usual on time as we assembled for the 6 am start. Many of the residents were also there to wave farewell to Bapak, some still in their housecoats at that early hour. Luggage was loaded into a new VW Combi wagon which has been sent by the Subud groups in Germany.

Usman was driving Bapak's car, with Bapak and Ibu sitting together in the back and Aminah (Usman's wife) in the front. The idea was to drive in a convoy. Haryono and Ismana with their family (on a mattress in the back) were first to follow Bapak's car. The Chairman of the National Committee, Commodore Sutanto, with his wife were next and with them Tuti, Muti and Indra, (Bapak's granddaughters). Members of the National Committee, Wahana and Sudono, together with Usman's children were in the new Combi. In the fourth car was Ashadikun and his wife and children and his brother. Ashadikun is an active member of the National Committee and the SES Representative of Indonesia. He is combining this trip with a business trip to sugar factories in East Java.

In the last two cars were Oswald Lake and his wife Asa from the USA with their two boys in the secretariat's old Chevrolet station wagon, and Erling Week, an American business man who had come to live in Cilandak at Bapak's invitation, Dr George Baerveldt, a visitor from South Africa, and Helena and I, in our car. We were in all twenty-two adults and as many children in seven cars.

We wove our way through the Jakarta traffic to the main bypass, then through some twenty kilometres of suburbs strung out along the coast road to the east. It was a narrow two lane road crowded with bicycles, rickshaws and pedestrians, as well as trucks and all manner of other vehicles bringing goods and people to Jakarta. Although we were early the going was slow and after an hour and a half we were still in the built-up area. It made me realise why it was going to take us all day to drive the five hundred kilometres to Semarang.

The convoy seemed to have a life of it's own as it sped along. Bapak's car led the cavalcade almost all the way, with the rest of the cars changing position from time to time. There was the usual urging by the children to pass their friends. There was some doubt about the old Chevrolet but it performed well. In fact no one had car problems although more than a hundred kilometres of the road was very rough, with large pot holes. In some places our speed was reduced to walking pace. Around midday we wound down from the hills towards the northern coastal plain. Stretched out below was a vast patchwork of paddy fields as far as one could see. It was mostly intense green mature rice, but here and there were vivid splashes of yellow seed rice and a few contrasting fallow ponds of rich brown soil edged with straw where groups of women in bright batiks were weeding and planting. We stopped to stretch our legs in this fertile place. A wide canal ran beside the road full to the top of its banks from the recent rains. Ibu walked with Aminah, her pink parasol aloft. A clear blue sky stretched to the horizon ahead.

Our next stop was for a late lunch at Tegal. Then more driving across the plains in the afternoon heat, until we came—with some relief—to the shady teak forests on the hills of Pekalongan. We arrived in Semarang just after dark.

We went directly to Bapak's house where his mother and Rahayu welcomed us. We all found chairs and were served cool drinks. Bapak explained that it was here that he first received God's Grace in the form of the Subud latihan. He also told us a little about the history of Semarang and how several centuries ago there had been a land promontory running out into the sea. In those days it was the meeting place of the Nine Walis (Saints) of Java. Just sitting with Bapak took away all the fatigue of the twelve hour drive. He was attentive, asking about our hotel accommodation and said that tomorrow we would rest.

Monday 29 December 1969

SEMARANG. I overslept this morning and arrived around 11 am at Bapak's house. Everyone was already there sitting around in a relaxed manner. It reminded me of those Christmas days at home when all the family gathered, totally at ease. Bapak's sister and her husband came with their children, then Bapak's younger brother. This meant that, with the exception of Hardiyati and her children, who had stayed in Cilandak to look after Bapak's house, the whole of Bapak's family—four generations—were here for Hari Raya Lebaran (the feast to celebrate the end of the fast).

Now one by one, from the youngest children of three years old through to the oldest relations, members of the family paid their respects to Bapak and to Eyang (Bapak's mother), each kneeling and touching their elder's knee with their folded hands. It was done in reverence and received with love.

In the evening we dressed in our new clothes (according to the custom at the end of Ramadhan) the men in suits and the women in kain and kebaya (sarong and lace blouse), and gathered again at Bapak's house. Ibu called all the ladies into her bedroom to see how they looked. We then followed Bapak to a large upstairs hall in the city centre where the group had invited him to give a talk. There were about one hundred and fifty members seated in rows as in a theatre. Pak Slamet was the respected elder.

It turned out that the group was using the occasion of Bapak's visit to elect a new chairman with the main task of preparing the Semarang group to host the Indonesian National Congress in 1971—a big job for a small group. When asked, Bapak declined to test the new chairman, short cutting the procedure by saying that he could see that he was suitable. We were then all served an evening meal.

In his talk Bapak gave clarifications about the aim and purpose of Subud. He said that we each have the responsibility for our own progress. Our mistakes and sufferings are due to our own situation, but this can be alleviated and made right by God's Grace.

I taped the talk for the Cilandak Tape Unit, who have given me their equipment to record all Bapak's talks on this trip. These will be translated and sent to ISC in UK. I enjoy doing the taping as I get to sit close to Bapak while he is talking and so can enter into the feeling and follow more closely what he is saying.

Tuesday 30 December 1969

TRETES. Yesterday Sutanto announced a change of plan. Instead of us staying one night in each place that Bapak is visiting, we would go to Tretes near Malang for two nights and make the journeys to the Surabaya and Malang groups from there. Similarly in Central Java we are to spend three nights in Yogyakarta and visit the groups in Solo and Temanggung from that base.

We made a late start this morning then drove to Solo, a hundred kilometres of winding mountain road. Although it was only 11 am when we arrived, we stopped at a restaurant in the gardens at the City Recreation Centre and had our midday meal. It turned out that Bapak's family had started the journey without taking breakfast. I think Ibu (who has diabetes) had not been so well the night before. The feeling between us all is now very close. Rahayu has joined us in our car.

The drive from Semarang to Surabaya via Solo and Madiun must be one of the most beautiful in Java. After leaving Solo the road runs along a wide fertile valley dominated by huge volcanic peaks. At first the volcanoes appeared grouped together and then as we approached them they separated into a line of three distinct mountains. The colours were striking, particularly in the late afternoon from 4 pm to sunset. At that time of day the towering cones became blue-black against the orange sky. The huge cumulus clouds of the monsoon reflected the sunset and transformed the green forests and fields into shades of purples. It was twilight as we turned off the main road in the direction of Mount Bromo and started climbing through farmlands towards the holiday resort of Tretes. In those magical minutes the landscape became translucent. A cluster of lights of the township could be seen sparkling like a tiara on the velvet black volcano.

Bapak, Ibu and family were accommodated in the main house of an Indonesian Navy Rest Centre and the rest of us were given rooms in the bungalows of the tourist hotel next door. We had been ten hours on the road, so with another sixty kilometres to drive to Surabaya ahead of us, we quickly showered and changed. Time and distance have become unimportant; we were now attuned to the spirit of a Bapak journey.

Surabaya is the site of Indonesia's Navy headquarters and the meeting tonight was arranged in the large Navy assembly hall. About a hundred and fifty members attended. I guess some are from other Subud centres. After the welcoming speeches, Bapak gave a talk lasting two hours. He said that the Association Susila Budhi Dharma had no existence apart from us, its members, and so Subud's progress and reputation rested with our progress and diligence. (Bapak often makes this point, to draw people's attention back to the fact that Subud is only an expression of the individual latihans of all of us.)

Bapak told the creation story as given in the Islamic holy books. He then went on to explain that the original light of creation divided into the four basic elements and that these re-combined to become the life forces of our world. We can, he said, experience the difference between these forces which make up our passions (nafsu) and the higher force of the latihan.

Wednesday 31 December 1969

TRETES. As we drove back to Tretes last night in the early hours all I remember was the closeness of the feeling between us in the car, and the echo of our hard-driven motors along the empty roads. This morning I could see the beauty of Tretes in daylight. From high on the mountain side, a vast soft blue-green plain spreads out below, while close at hand is a mass of brightly-coloured gardens. Temperate as well as tropical plants grow well here and the holiday houses are thickly planted with flowering trees and shrubs. Mid-morning Bapak and Ibu went for a walk to Haryono's bungalow. We followed and joined the relaxed and laughing group sitting listening to Bapak tell stories in joking mood. Some children were there, others had gone riding.

Thursday 1 January 1970

TRETES. Last night (New Year's Eve) and again this evening we went to the Malang group with Bapak. Both times Bapak gave a two hour talk to about a hundred members. After the talk on New Year's Eve a Javanese gamelan orchestra played and one by one people got up and sang.

Tonight we had latihan and afterwards Bapak did testing. Bapak encouraged the group to get their own premises. I feel that Bapak is using the example of Subud abroad to encourage the Indonesian members to improve their situation. 'Bapak will come again (only) when you have a latihan hall, but don't take longer than a year!' he said.

This mountainous area of Malang has a temperate climate and is famous in Java for apples and tobacco. This morning we bought apples to take back to friends in Cilandak, where they are a great luxury in the Jakarta market. Because there is no autumn season the orchardists have to pull the leaves off by hand. As the trip progresses our station wagon and other cars are filling up with the overflow of Ibu's packages. She is the Great Mother, always collecting and giving.

Friday 2 January 1970

YOGYAKARTA. We started early this morning for the three hundred kilometres drive from Tretes to Yogyakarta and made good time, arriving in Solo before lunch. Solo, the popular name for Surakarta, was in early times the capital of one of the old kingdoms of Java and enjoyed a high culture. To this day the people have a reputation for their refinement and almost excessive courtesy. The Solo group entertained us for lunch at the home of one of the members, an elegant old-style house with an elevated verandah shaded by a huge tree.

Bapak was obviously at home talking with old friends, while some of our party admired pusaka (heirlooms), kris (daggers) and other ceremonial weapons, prized for their magical powers, in the house of our host. The women brought and traded beautiful batiks. Everyone wore traditional clothes, adding to the ambience of a former era. It was as if little had changed for hundreds of years.

Bapak and his family have been accommodated in four flats in a modern guesthouse. We the foreigners (as we are called) and the National Committee are housed in a smaller guest house nearby. It is close enough for us to take part in Bapak's hour-to-hour activities.

After the greetings we showered and changed and drove back to Solo for Bapak's talk. The group's hall was filled to capacity—at least a hundred and fifty people were seated and more standing behind. I noticed many young people in the men's group. Bapak gave a two hour talk and afterwards some testing, restricted to a few of the women because of the space. The visit ended long after midnight.

Saturday 3 January 1970

YOGYAKARTA. Today was a rest day. We went to the station and booked a seat for Erling who has to return to Jakarta, then came back via the shops so he could buy presents. Yogyakarta is famous for its batiks and silverware, both ornaments and household ware.

Yogyakarta is flat but from the city you see the mountains, particularly the three thousand metre peak of Mount Merapi, an active volcano. I remember that as recently as last year it erupted, causing several villages to be evacuated as lava poured down its slopes. The city is the old capital of Java and was the centre of one of the great Javanese kingdoms of earlier times. It has an atmosphere of past greatness and present mystery.

Bapak's talk to the Yogyakarta group tonight was held in the hall next to the guesthouse. First we had latihan in a part screened off for the purpose. It seemed to me that Bapak's talk was particularly warm and cordial, reflecting his close connection with this group. It was a large hall with plenty of space to spread mats for testing between Bapak and the audience. Bapak called two groups of twenty women, one after the other, then two groups of about the same number of men. The testing was (as we have had in Cilandak) to show to what extent the various parts of the body have been purified.

Sunday 4 January 1970

YOGYAKARTA. This morning Bapak and Ibu went out for a drive and invited us to join them. The road to the beach was impassable, so Bapak decided to go to the hill station of Kali-Urang on the slopes of Mt. Merapi. This was a series of holiday bungalows and restaurants popular for the cool mountain climate. We had a most enjoyable morning relaxing and strolling around the roads of this colourful place. Rahayu bought us omelettes filled with spicy vegetables from a roadside stall set up for Sunday tourists, while some of the ladies walked with Ibu to see a waterfall. In the evening we visited the group at the town of Temanggung.

Our group is now noticeably reduced since most of the children have returned to Jakarta to start school tomorrow. Some went by train and some in the Combi.

Temanggung is very close to Wolono, where Ibu was born. It is a medium size town almost half way between Yogyakarta and Semarang. Two hundred members gathered from various groups in the district and gave Bapak and Ibu a extremely loving welcome. We were treated to a meal and then Bapak gave a talk. Many of the members here are rural people and Bapak spoke almost tenderly—no wonder everyone loves him! Because of the hospitality and because of the long return journey, there was no time for testing.

When we got back this evening Usman said the arrangements for Bandung had been changed. After the talk tomorrow night Bapak will drive on, either to Tjipanas (Bapak's house halfway to Jakarta) or go through to Jakarta.

Monday 5 January 1970

JAKARTA. Yesterday morning we took the southern road out of Yogyakarta towards Bandung. The country was flat and dry yet seemed to be densely populated. The crops were corn, dry rice and millet. Rahayu said that millet—djuwawut—was Java's original staple food, from which the island gets it's name. The land holdings were small, very different to the large wet rice paddies in the north.

As we approached the coast we came upon large coconut plantations. The roads were narrow and crowded with bicycles and horse-drawn vehicles, mostly four-wheel buggies. There were few motor vehicles and our convoy, now six cars, had constantly to sound a warning to the slow local traffic.

Two hours from Yogyakarta we arrived at Purworedjo, where Bapak had been invited to give a short talk. I stopped for petrol and arrived late to find Bapak already sitting down before a group of about fifty members.

The building was the Kabupaten, the formal residence of the Regent. The architecture was impressive, in the traditional style of the old Javanese aristocracy, and set in gardens with a sweep of lawns and driveway to the entrance. There was a large semi-open front reception hall about twenty meters square with a high ceiling and low walls, known as the pendopo. Its fine low angle roof was supported on four carved wooden columns in the middle of the tiled floor space. Behind this was a hallway opening into a more intimate reception room in the form of a T. It was here that Bapak had been welcomed. Behind this were the private living quarters.

About thirty of the members were sitting in front of Bapak and the remainder on the two sides. Many of those in front were government functionaries and military personnel. I judged they were high-ranking persons by the brass on their uniforms. The Bupati (Regent) sat in the group on Bapak's right. He was the civil administrator of the district. In earlier times, I was told, the Regent was related to the royal family of that kingdom. Nowadays he was a person trained in a special school for public affairs. Everyone looked immaculately dressed except we travel-worn foreigners!

I set up the tape recorder while light refreshments were served. Bapak began his talk very quietly and intimately, leaning forward towards the party, gathering them into the feeling of his explanation. I was captivated by the intimacy Bapak created. His talk was the essence of refinement, a masterpiece of nuance and elegant gesture. The effect (as I experienced it) was to make us feel that we were special people, privileged to be at this gathering.

After a brief farewell, we quickly settled down to fast driving for the long journey to Bandung. It was 3 pm before we stopped for lunch at a restaurant in a small country town. There was no sign of the Chevrolet station wagon with Oswald and Asa and Dr George. As we left the restaurant I lost sight of Bapak's car and for the rest of the day we drove somewhere behind the convoy, concerned to catch up as I had no address to go to in Bandung—a city of several million people.

The mountains of West Java were no less beautiful than those we saw in the East, but different. The road wound through red soil hillsides of tilled cassava crops and brilliant green valleys of rice terraces, and on every horizon that enchanting soft blue-green haze of Java that makes near hills look distant and mysterious.

It was well after dark when we arrived in Bandung. Luckily, by asking someone, we found our way to a large brightly-lit hall just two minutes before Bapak began his talk. When I heard that we were to drive another five hours tonight back to Jakarta I gave the tape recorder to Dr George and, following Usman's example, stole out to the car for a sleep. Just after midnight Bapak emerged and waved farewell to the crowd of some two hundred members. Our small convoy slipped easily along the quiet roads through Bogor to Jakarta. At 5 am Bapak and Ibu stepped lightly into their front sitting room and we, tired but happy, dissolved into our houses.

...

In October 1970 Bapak left Cilandak for his fourth around-the-world journey visiting thirty groups in twenty countries and travelling for three and a half months. Soon after his return in February 1971 Ibu died. Although she had not been in good health her death was totally unexpected and a great shock to everyone. Ibu was beloved of all Subud women and deeply missed. Her passing marked the end of a unique relationship between the Big House and the women residents of Cilandak. It was also the end of an era of cultural life in the compound which was based on Javanese tradition which Ibu had sustained.

...

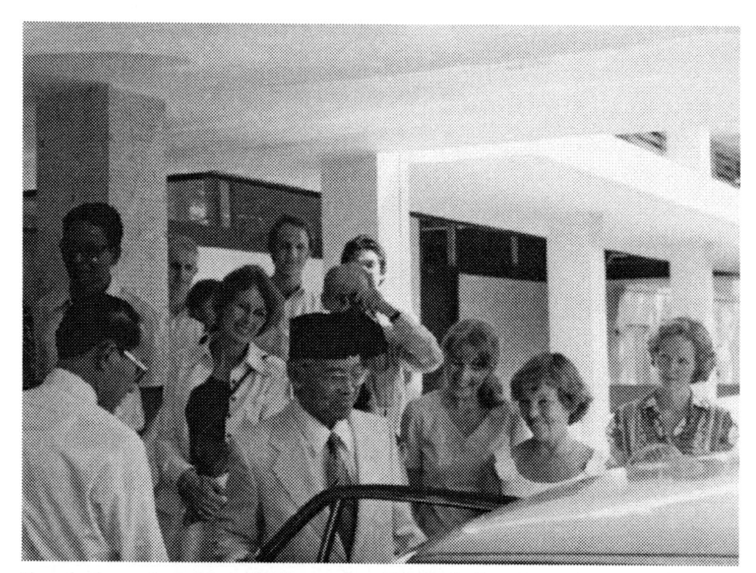

Bapak departing from his house in Cilandak for the 1970 World Tour

Bapak talking with members in Spain 1970, Istimah Week translating

While Bapak was travelling, Ramzi, Abdullah and I were busy with the work of a growing business. We gave our firm the name International Design Consultants (IDC) to emphasise our overseas skills and our advisory role, as distinct from designer-builders. Ramzi and Abdullah continued to expand their contacts—Ramzi had been working as supervising architect on the new German Embassy and Abdullah had been assisting with the construction stage of the Australian Embassy—and I began to set up the client agreements and the procedures for letting and managing building contracts. These had to be based on a combination of Indonesian practice, international terms of contract, and our own specifications and costing information. Fortunately our first job at the Australian Ambassador's residence was small, giving us the opportunity to gain experience with local contractors and costs.

We also needed time to become accustomed to the practical difficulties of building in Jakarta at that time. The infrastructure had failed—public electricity and water supply served only part of the population and often broke down, telephones did not work, roads were in disrepair and were regularly flooded in times of heavy rain. The economy was bankrupt and the chaotic political situation of recent times simmered under the surface making important decisions by government officials subject to endless delays. There was a serious lack of trained tradesmen in all areas.

In 1968 IDC began to get factory projects for foreign investors. The company started to grow as clients recommended us to others. The next year, at Bapak's suggestion, Haryono and Wahono joined us as non-working directors and we made application to the Indonesian Government to form a joint venture company under the Foreign Investment Law.

Up until this time Abdullah, Ramzi and I worked together on every project and on all the administration issues faced by the practice. This period of sharing everything was very important and built the basis for our personal cooperation in the years to come when we had to divide up the work.

(Left to right) Lamaan van Sommers, Abdullah Pope and Ramzi Winkler

PT IDC office next door to Wisma Subud in Cilandak 1970

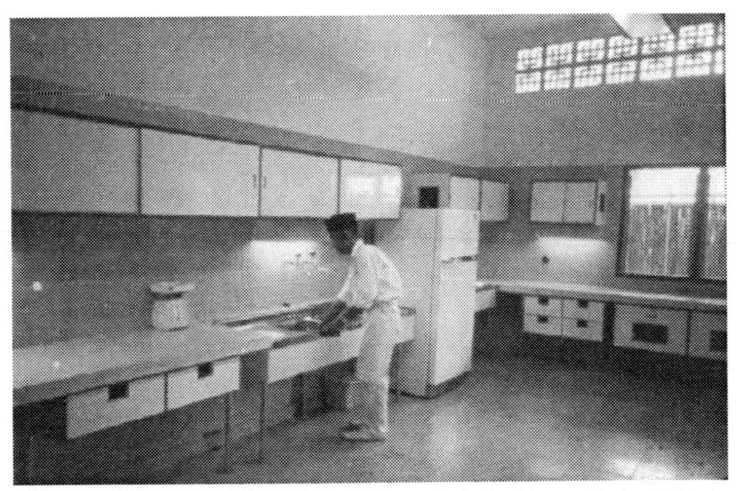

PT IDC's first project: Australian Ambassador's Residence kitchen 1968

PT IDC's first factory project in Jakarta 1968

Joint Embassy School (later renamed Jakarta International School)
Architecture by Abdullah Pope, PT IDC

Joint Embassy School Gymnasium and Assembly Hall by PT IDC

As the number of projects increased, we followed the expectation of our clients to deal with one director—designated the 'director-in-charge' of their project—and divided up the work. We continued to attend the initial meetings with new clients together, and it was here that the latihan noticeably helped us to establish good working relationships with strangers from many countries. We had a tacit agreement that we should arrive in a quiet inner state and then consciously support each other when we spoke, by remembering our latihan state. Clients invariably left our office satisfied and often with some comment like, 'How quiet and peaceful it is here.'

Although we now portioned out the work, my feeling of responsibility for the whole did not diminish. It usually fell to me to worry through the contract clauses with the lawyers of American companies who were not familiar with the UK 'Conditions of Contract', which we always used. I took an interest in everything and was always ready to back up the staff. We were like a growing family, particularly when new employees came to us untrained. Where projects were demanding I became meticulous about how things should be done in the name of IDC. I had the highest regard for the company and felt that it enhanced the name of Subud. I felt that what I was doing was for IDC and what my partners also did was a gift to the company. I delighted in everyone's achievements. All these things flowed naturally from the latihan.

Bapak's role was advisory. He was there if the partners wanted his advice, but he didn't lead. We occasionally asked him about matters of policy and about the work we were doing in Cilandak. At Board meetings Bapak left it to us to set the agenda. He would take an interest in what was said, commenting when asked or showing his assent to our discussions. The effect of his presence was to bring out the best in us. When my partners spoke at these meetings, I was filled with gratitude to God *that I was sharing this experience, at this moment, with these people.*

By the end of 1969 IDC had established technical departments responsible to the three directors: Abdullah and Ramzi had an architecture group, under Pak Umar*, and I had a structural engineering section, under Ir Soetikno†, and a small quantity surveying team, under Pak Hartono. This was a time when I spent much of each day with my staff. They were dedicated to IDC and eager to do well at their jobs. They were reliable, punctual and never absent. It was a time of training, of establishing methodology and of fostering skills. They learnt quickly and produced excellent work. They were a happy and harmonious team. I felt at home when working with them and discovered that my willingness to take responsibility gave them, as technical people, confidence and security. There grew a strong bond of affection between us which the latihan protected from declining into over-familiarity.

Meantime on Bapak's advice we bought the land alongside Wisma Subud to build an office and staff houses. Ramzi and I and Lambert Gibbs, an English architect who had joined IDC, began building our houses in 1970. At the same time Irwan Maindonald, an experienced mechanical and electrical engineer from New Zealand, decided to set up a building services consultancy, which he called Asian Area Consultants (AAC) and rented the house next door—between Bapak's house and IDC. In Indonesia at that time the public utilities were inadequate to meet any extra demand, so every new factory or building had to provide its own electricity generators, its own water supply, and its own waste treatment system. AAC engineers designed these services as well as air-conditioning, telecommunications, and fire protection systems for the factories, schools and office buildings handled by IDC. AAC became vital to IDC, as it complemented the architecture and engineering of sophisticated projects. In January 1970 Irwan asked me to recruit staff for AAC and manage the business. I worked as managing director for two years until he came to live fulltime in Indonesia. This meant that I was dividing my time between IDC and AAC.

* Pak is an abbreviation for Bapak. † Ir is the title for a qualified engineer.

During all this period we enjoyed both the confidence of being under Bapak's guidance and the optimism that pervaded business life in Indonesia at the time.

Towards the end of 1970, Bapak began to prepare Cilandak to host the Fourth Subud World Congress in August 1971. Although IDC was occupied with the design of several large factory projects, office buildings and the Joint Embassy School, we took on the extensive preparations for the Congress. Sharif designed a new latihan hall and Ramzi Winkler designed and supervised construction of temporary accommodation for 1500 guests built entirely of bamboo. I was responsible for the electricity and water supplies, including installing new generators and drilling a deep bore to an aquifer of potable water.

The Congress was attended by over 2000 members from more than 50 countries making it the largest international gathering ever held in Indonesia. President Suharto, Ministers and the Mayor of Jakarta were invited, bringing Subud to the attention of the nation through the media.

As IDC expanded, financing became critical and we had to look for loans as working capital. Sharif Horthy, who had meantime joined us as an engineer, now provided much-needed finance. On 27 June 1970, with the help of Erling Week, acting as IDC managing director, we obtained the President's signature approving our application to operate in Indonesia. In November when Erling left, I took over as managing director, so that for several months I was deeply absorbed in staff matters, financial control and company administration for both companies. Money was short. The company had no bank credit and was depending increasingly on private loans to meet the cash flow requirements of its expanding business. In June of the following year Sharif became a shareholder of IDC and was appointed managing director. I returned to the technical direction of a pharmaceutical factory for Bristol-Myers and a factory and offices for Danapaints. By this time IDC and AAC were ready for a much larger project.

The new latihan hall designed by Sharif Horthy PT IDC 1971

Awaiting the arrival of President Suharto at the opening of Congress 1971

The van Sommers' house adjacent to the IDC office in Wisma Subud

The Winklers' house on IDC land (later part of Wisma Subud)

In December 1972 IDC and AAC were appointed by the Canadian mining company International Nickel (PT INCO in Indonesia) to produce a design report and contract drawings for a township to be built near the village of Soroako on the shore of Lake Matano in a remote area of the island of Sulawesi. It was to include a staff town of 600 houses, schools, hospital, supermarket, clubs, roads and all utilities, and serviced lots for 1000 local employees, growing to a population of 8000 in ten years. I became the director responsible, with Lambert as architect and with Irwan taking care of the utilities. It was the chance of a lifetime—total freedom for planning, layout, building details and materials on a virgin site in a beautiful location. We had no town planning experience but were able to use the topography of the undulating terrain and tree cover to suggest a certain arrangement. We chose the flatter areas for the town centre and sports fields and used aerial photographs to lay out the roads according to the contours. As we grouped the houses to take advantage of the lake views, it became clear that we had not succeeded in creating a functional town centre. We had not resolved this problem when Lambert suffered a heart attack and had to withdraw from the project.

In May 1973 Fernando Davanzo, an architect from Chile, visited Cilandak and I asked him if he could help us with the project. The timing was remarkable. Fernando was experienced in social planning of remote communities and he immediately took Lambert's place. In the next three months he helped develop a successful town plan around his concept of using the schools as centres of educational, cultural and recreational activity for adults as well as children. Here is how he described his work with IDC in an later interview:

> I had worked in Chile on schemes to meet the social needs of isolated work forces. The principle was to extend the role of schools so that they became centres for family activity and adult learning out of normal school hours. My idea was to apply this principle to the INCO township.

IDC was to prepare a presentation of their approach to the township design for the head of INCO engineering who was arriving from Toronto that month. We set out to draw a five metres long layout of the town to scale. The housing was divided into two distinct areas: the management at the far end where the land sloped to the lake, and the workers nearer the mine where the land was flatter. There was a large park and sports fields connecting them.

A glow of exhilaration surrounded the work at IDC. With a very tight program we called on women in the Subud compound to help colour-wash the large drawings. These volunteers included: Halimah Geiger (later Mrs Russ); Shirley, wife of Musa Djoemena; Toti, my wife; Renée (from Germany); Latifah (later Mrs Asikin); Sylvia des Tombe; and a daughter of Dr Rachman Mitchell. We finished the proposed layout the night before the arrival of INCO's chief engineer, Mr Crouch.

Our strategy was to emphasise the social dimension on which the ultimate success of the town, and therefore the project, would depend. The school was to be the community centre—the hall for school assembly would be used for cinema and theatre; classrooms would be open for adult education and interest groups; the library for the school would be combined with a public lending and reference library; tennis courts, sports fields and swimming pools, etc. would be managed for both school and residents' use, and all these activities would be organised and run by the residents. Mr Crouch saw that the emphasis was right and was happy with the ideas. He instructed us to continue along these lines and said he would come back in a month. It was clear that IDC had been selected as the consultant.

We settled down to perfect the layout and prepare the descriptions of the buildings—the schools, supermarkets, clubs, hospital, mosque and churches, and the township offices. INCO began to send their staff to consult with us; a young American woman teacher about the schools, a Japanese doctor to discuss the hospital and clinic requirements. The IDC architects developed house designs and the engineers prepared building systems, using locally milled timber.

Meantime Lamaan, Soetikno and I flew to the Sulawesi site. It was on the shore of Lake Matano, a huge deep freshwater lake surrounded by a pristine landscape of hills and bushland. We used an STOL aircraft, which could fly very slowly, for observations that would help us adjust our layout. In the sloping area, the location of roads and buildings was determined largely by the land contours, giving the plan a settled and natural appearance.

Back in Jakarta I worked on designing the schools, the supermarket, and the hospital. Lamaan arranged for staff architects to work on the various house types and other buildings, and his engineers designed the roads and recreation areas. The draftsmen made a two-metre long scale model. We worked very hard, sometimes until 2 am, and then returned early the next morning—some staff did not go home but slept at the office—so as to finish the plan before I left for Chile. Many things had to be considered, including the impact of the mine on the people of Soroako village, the port township Malili, and the island of Sulawesi as a whole.

When Fernando returned to Chile I was left to prepare a detailed report suitable for INCO to use in going out to tender for construction of the township. As the end of year deadline approached I slept little, working day and night for the last several weeks to complete a description of the town and its buildings, illustrated with scores of drawings and specifications. I worked until I thought the last drop of energy was gone, and then I went on. The surprising result was that I passed through the fatigue and—*feeling totally at one with my own nature*—I was able to complete the extensive report and documentation on time. This was such a powerful spiritual experience that when it was complete I felt that I should present a copy to Bapak. I knew that he would understand.

The report was favourably received by INCO, and IDC was commissioned to carry out the detailed production drawings, specifications and bills of materials—to the last nail—for the project. It was IDC's and AAC's largest-ever project. To meet the program IDC expanded its staff to sixty-five and AAC to forty-five.

Fernando Davanzo (left) and IDC Chief Engineer Soetikno at INCO site

West end of the INCO new township, Sulawesi, designed by PT IDC

Robin Ripley (who later worked on the Anugraha Conference Centre in Windsor, England) came from the UK to design the timber housing construction system, a key element of the project. This was a time of prosperity for IDC and of satisfaction for the staff working on the project as they grew in experience and skill. By the time it was finished in August 1975 IDC had worked 30,000 manhours and AAC 20,000 manhours, completing six hundred detailed production drawings. The program involved thirty fulltime technical staff. With the team working efficiently and harmoniously the INCO project was for many the high point of IDC's first ten years. The township when built was one of the most modern in Indonesia.

The income from the INCO project carried the two companies through the initial effects of the 1975 Indonesian financial recession, and when it was completed, with most levels of staff competent to manage their own work, the directors had the chance to take their first significant holidays overseas.

The next large project for IDC was the structural engineering design of the S.Widjojo building, a fourteen storey office block on Jalan Sudirman in central Jakarta, initiated by Bapak. The architect for the building was Hassan Vogel, a Swiss Subud member who had had extensive experience of designing office buildings in Bangkok. IDC was responsible for the engineering. Java is a region of high earthquake activity and Jakarta is built on layers of water-logged silt. This meant that both the foundation system and the frame analysis would require the latest international design techniques. I employed specialists within Indonesia and from Australia. The Indonesian consultants, Luthfi and Associates, were invited to do the seismic analysis and to obtain the Government building permit. Matthew Shanley, a Subud engineer working in Perth with CMPS, an Australian company, conceived and developed the structural design. It was the first multi-storey building in Jakarta to be supported on a 'raft' foundation instead of on piles.

It was coincidental that this concept of 'floating' the building was consistent with its ship-like shape. I sent Sahlan, the senior draftsman, to Perth to work for three months at CMPS and on his return he and the others under Ir Soetikno did the structural drawings and reinforcement schedules.

The design process was a complete success and helped to establish the international competence of IDC's Indonesian engineering staff.

All this work activity was balanced by added attention to our inner life. Bapak continued to give talks on Sundays, sometimes to all members, at other times to the women helpers alone. He also gave talks at Ramadhan and to National Congresses, Zonal Conferences, and on all special occasions.

But life was by no means all work and prehatin (self denial). We regularly took weekend breaks. For some of us Samudra Beach Hotel on the south coast was a favourite destination.

The success of IDC during its first ten years went far beyond its important role in the development of Cilandak. It contributed to the economy of the country by building good quality factories, schools, housing and offices; it provided the study places for thousands of students in the schools and work places for hundreds of workers in the factories and offices; it gave a secure livelihood to a large technical staff and their families; and it set an example of good practice and honesty in the investment community of Jakarta.

PT IDC was founded by Bapak and those of us who worked as directors were related to one another through our relationship to Bapak and the latihan. Our reward was being near Bapak and the personal experience of working with brothers who, in Bapak's words, *'felt most comfortable close to latihan and who felt uncomfortable when, in what they were doing, they got away from the latihan'.*

S.Widjojo Building: architecture by Hassan Vogel, engineering by PT IDC

Samudra beach on Java south coast. Hotel pool in the foreground.

Left to right: Iliana Bartok, Erling and Istimah Week, Deanna Bartok, Hassanah van Sommers, Lestari Vittachi and son Imran, at Samudra.

Each year in Cilandak, like all residents, I followed the month-long Ramadhan fast. For three consecutive years I found myself in an outer situation that reinforced the experience of the fast. Each time, towards the end of the fast, when fasting had made me feel more sensitive to people's condition, I found myself in a place where the human situation was desperate. These synchronistic conjunctions of outer and inner events had a strong impact.

The first year I had to go to the slums of Jakarta because a servant was ill. I had never before been down the narrow walkways between the shacks built in the swamps. I felt moved with shame at the kindness and respect given to me by the family in the small and crowded servant's room. The second year I was asked to go to a hospice to give advice on building improvements. Ibrahim, a Subud member, had begun to pick up the dying from the streets and take them to this primitive hospice. He had only just started the project and the conditions were still much as he had found them. Gaunt people lay dying in bamboo shelters with only a cloth for cover. I had never had direct contact with such abject hopelessness.

The third year I was called to Sumatra to prepare a feasibility study for the development of Medan harbour on the north-east coast. The work was soil sampling on the tidal flats. This wide expanse of bare black mud, remote from the city, was home to the poor who couldn't find a shack in the city's slums. Dotted about in tiny temporary shelters to protect them from the pitiless tropical sun, these were forgotten people. Surely this was the last place on earth and yet these simple people had no where else to go. Still fasting, I worked the whole day deeply touched by their situation. I came away thankful to God for this experience of compassion.

...

In June 1975 I attended the Fifth Subud World Congress in Germany. It was well organised and very active, lasting eight days. Almost two thousand members attended. The venue was the Wolfsburg Civic Centre with plenary sessions held in its three-thousand-seat hall. The Congress was opened by the Mayor of Wolfsburg, who was then shown around an exhibition of Subud enterprise displays set up for the public in the foyer. IDC was represented. Most people were accommodated in the two-storey dormitory buildings in the permanent Volkswagon motor company village but some chose to stay, as I did, in one of the comfortable local inns. After the evening sessions we gathered in the coffee shops talking late into the night and eating German cakes.

Bapak was housed in the castle at Wendhausen, a beautiful old building in its own parklike grounds, half an hours' drive away from the congress venue. On his birthday all the members, many dressed in their national costumes, came to visit and pay their respects. Forming into a great line a kilometre long they filed past, country by country, each greeting Bapak and his family seated on a carpeted dais. Some, like the Germans, played music as they walked, some brought gifts.

In the evenings, Bapak gave talks and held latihans. I remember his analogies in his advice to the helpers. It is very important, he said, that we allow the latihan to move us according to our real nature. In that way our life will go well. If a goat acts like a tiger it will certainly not make a good tiger. In our latihan we should start relaxed and quiet so that we can follow the true movements according to our nature. The helpers should respect this. They should not interfere with a member's latihan, even if he barks like a dog. Through the latihan a person can come to know themselves. There were two evenings of testing with members. Each ended with showing how people of different races move and behave. How does a German walk? How does an American dance? The latihan was strong. Bapak said it was particularly good for newer members to be able to have a strong and clear experience.

The Fifth Subud World Congress, Wolfsburg, Germany, in session

Bapak at the Subud enterprise displays. PT IDC was one of sixty exhibits.

The third night of testing was for helpers. Bapak said that where Subud membership had fallen off, it was to some extent the responsibility of the helpers, so he would test how helpers should be. He asked us to receive:

Q. How does a person who will make a good helper feel to you? [Bapak: 'Like a father to his children.']

Q. How does a person who is not suitable to be a helper feel to you?

Some helpers made a big noise in this test and Bapak said, 'If you test like that in front of a candidate you will frighten them.' Then Bapak asked us to test about ourselves as helpers:

Q. How does it feel when you are acting with the correct attitude towards the members?

Q. How do you actually feel towards the members?

Q. Feel the quality which attracts the members towards you as a helper.

At the plenary sessions Bapak set the direction and the tone for each day by giving a short talk. On the third day he described the international organisation, with its two distinct sides—spiritual and committee. He announced that on the organisation side, Herbert Stewart from Toronto would head the International Subud Committee (ISC) for the next four years. On the spiritual side Bapak nominated two North American helpers to work beside ISC in Toronto and four others to advise Varindra Vittachi, who would be 'Bapak's assistant on organisational matters.' Bapak also said he would send Roespono, a helper from Indonesia, to live in Canada. He confirmed that members of Bapak's secretariat had no position in the running of Subud. He outlined the guidelines for Subud enterprise contributions and the use of funds for helper travel, and so on. It was a very comprehensive congress.

After Germany I had the impulse to travel through the Americas. It turned out to be an odyssey of Subud visits where I shared with others the events and substance of the World Congress and showed slides. I went to groups in Santiago, Chile; Buenos Aires, Argentina;

Rio de Janerio, Brazil; Lima, Peru; Toronto and Vancouver, Canada; and Albuquerque, Flagstaff and San Francisco in the USA.

In Chile I stayed two weeks. The group arranged an evening for the congress report and finished with questions about life in Cilandak. I visited a farm where Latif Petric and three other members were working hard to establish a cheese making enterprise.

In Lima I stayed five days with Eduardo and Anna Massini, the Kejiwaan Councillors for Peru. The group was small but we met several times for latihan and dined out together. One night at a restaurant we were laughing and enjoying ourselves so much that the waiters, after standing all the spare chairs on the tables, finally had to turn off the lights to get us out. In Mexico City I stayed with Hosanna Baron, who had been several times to Cilandak, and with her visited the ancient Aztec pyramids. It was here in her house in the grounds of Chapultepec Golf Club in 1968 that Bapak had a strong receiving which caused a number of people to have visions and other extraordinary spiritual experiences.*

In New York Varindra and Lestari Vittachi invited me to dinner. Lestari was our neighbour and close friend in Cilandak in the days when Imran was a small boy and Varindra had had to spend much of his time elsewhere. Varindra was at the time director of information and public affairs for the UN Population Fund and arranged for me to visit the United Nations building and Security Council chamber as a tourist. In Toronto I went to see Herbert Stewart, who had been appointed ISC Chairman at the Wolfsburg Congress. We did latihan and tested together about his coming task.

Everything went so well during this journey and people were so appreciative of getting first hand news of the World Congress that I felt quite sure that my impulse to travel had been a right indication. In between the group visits I had the chance to travel to the famous tourist sites of Brazilia, Machu Picchu and Cusco in Peru, Mexico City, New York, Niagara Falls, the Rocky Mountains National Parks, the Grand Canyon and Hawaii.

* See account by Lydia Duncan in *Subud Journal* 1968

On 14 February 1976 my mother died in Melbourne. She had been bravely battling a long illness. She had been in Subud fourteen years and, thanks to God, I was able to be with her for the last three weeks of her life. As I sat beside her bed I received very emphatically the word, ' ... indestructible.' I understood that in the state of latihan that I was sharing with her there was a part of her which would not be wiped out by death. When the time came for her to die I felt assured in my latihan that she left gladly and that she was in God's care. I wrote to Bapak, who had recently given my mother the new name Maria.

At forty-eight

Back in Jakarta, I found IDC struggling to find new projects in a national economy critically short of foreign investment due to the oil shock of 1973. With no significant work and the engineering division functioning well without my supervision, I decided to retire and leave Indonesia. It felt as natural to leave as it had been to join. I had been drawn into the possibilities of IDC at its inception and helped it grow to maturity and self-sufficiency. Now my contribution was complete.I told Bapak of my decision and he agreed. On 30 April, at forty-eight years of age I resigned from the company. I parted with mixed feelings. I knew it was the right thing to do but I also felt very close to my engineering staff and left them with enormous goodwill.

While my years in Indonesia and my time with IDC had given me great satisfaction in my spiritual and professional life, the same cannot be said of my marriage, which had foundered in the last years and finished in separation in 1975. As the financial situation at IDC had declined, I had to settle with no retirement benefit. This meant that I left Indonesia with very little capital to start a new life. This didn't bother me at the time. I had enjoyed such a rich spiritual experience that I never thought to measure my ten-year stay in Indonesia in terms of money.

At first I felt that I would like to live in Canada, but when I told Bapak he advised me to return to Australia.

~

Postscript 1976

The inner changes that led to my leaving Indonesia were to continue. From that time on my interests were radically different. I was drawn to matters of feeling in preference to thinking, to inner things rather than outer, to relationships rather than projects and achievements, and I entered into life with a new optimism.

As I prepared to leave Indonesia, I had a dramatic spiritual experience, which was to strengthen my move to independence.

One day I was moved to lie down and to do the latihan. With it came clear consciousness and a blissful feeling. I was inwardly separated—an observer. As the feeling and the separation intensified, my *self* was suddenly beside me. He was a very large figure, several times life size, towering over me to the left and above. He looked down on me, knowingly, as apparently my *self* had always done. I looked up at him in awe. No recognition was necessary, as it was *me*, but I was amazed. It was wonderful to meet *him*. There was so much more to him than I. He was more *real* than I. Being me, he knew all about me and was constantly aware of what I was doing. When moments later he was gone I was left thrilled with the wonder of the experience. My reaction was to want to find *his* plane of consciousness but gradually I had to accept that I could not. The important thing was that I was changed by the experience. I was reassured of a substantial and eternal dimension to my existence, even if I was usually cut off from it.

~

Part Two

~

Chapter Seven

Helper Activities

A month had past since I arrived in Perth. I still enjoyed feelings of wellbeing and confidence for the future, although in reality I had made little progress towards a new career. I felt as if I was on extended leave from my work in Indonesia. This emphasis on leisure time was most obvious in my routine of early rising to answer correspondence or read a growing collection of new books. By staying up after the Moslem dawn prayer I had four hours to myself before breakfast.

Yesterday's letter from Emilia lay on my writing desk. Emilia was a Subud helper who had frequently visited my mother during her last months in hospital. As a result of their closeness we had kept in touch. As was my custom I had read her letter immediately it arrived. The feelings it evoked returned again and again throughout the day. Now I would answer it, searching for the stillness of my feelings where an insight might bring some resolution to the unfolding drama that I had come to share with my Subud sister, two thousand kilometres away. It was 4.00 a.m.

Now and then, when the flow of my letter writing slowed, I would leave the study and take a walk outside, as Bapak had once advised me at the IDC office: 'Get up and walk around a little, loosen up those shoulders!' he said. I remembered too how he wrote that as a young man in Semarang he would take late night walks after study. Now I sought the fresh air, to clear my head. I walked on the brick paving around the pool, staying close to the wall that blocked the light of the single distant street lamp so I could see the wonder of the night sky. It was translucent in that dry climate, the great arc of the Milky Way revealed in all its splendour.

How different from the dark blue velvet sky of tropical Jakarta, I thought, now far away to the north, *and how different is this Australian city's silence to Jakarta's wakeful sounds of early morning, with its distant calls to prayer.*

I sat at my desk and re-read Emilia's letter.

June 1, 1976

Dear Lamaan,

Of all Subud people, you perhaps know me best. Yet even you cannot imagine my agony of mind. I would not wish that you should. Why should you suffer? It does not solve anything. My problem is that I have absolute confidence in the latihan and yet the large Subud enterprises show serious signs of failure. Where is the mistake?

I go over and over the options. The truth is that there is no answer in the arrangement and rearrangement of the facts available to my thinking. I ask the latihan for more guidance but—on this issue— I can find no resolution.

You might say, from the viewpoint of idealism, (or perhaps the dogmatism of a Subud member?) that the choice is obvious— I should have faith that all will work out right in the end. I agree with you, my trust in the latihan and in Bapak is unquestionable. That is the problem—it is *also* the latihan that is pushing me to trust in my own feelings, and my feelings say that all is not well.

The result is that I am now split in anguish between two states of honour. I begin to have two selves. They alternately take the high ground of the argument. And the energy of this inner conflict even manifests in my dreams. Day and night the struggle for my soul has continued over these recent months with little respite.

But now, dear brother, into this turmoil has come an explanation like a ray of light in the darkness. I have found someone who understands my experience and has given it a totally new significance.

It happened like this.

Soon after we came back to New Zealand and moved into this our new house in Auckland, your family sent me two of your mother's books. They seem to have been oddments in her library. One was by Khrisnamurti, the other *Memories, Dreams and Reflections* by CG Jung. I knew of Khristnamurti's writings but was surprised because your mother never mentioned him. Regarding Jung, all I knew was that he was a Swiss psychologist. I had never read his writings. I put the books away and had forgotten them until a few days ago, when I heard Jung's name mentioned on the radio. Something clicked and I felt I should find the book.

I was soon engrossed in it and continued reading the following day. Towards the end, to my joy, I came to a description of my situation—how it can happen to a person that circumstances in life can present them with an impossible choice. When both issues are equally driven by a sense of duty, deeply held, they may well enter into a state of inner conflict with no way out. This is the excerpt:

> ... if a man faced with a conflict of duties undertakes to deal with them absolutely on his own responsibility, and before a judge who sits in judgment on him day and night, he may well find himself in an isolated position. There is now an authentic secret in his life which cannot be discussed—if only because he is involved in an endless inner trial in which he is his own counsel and ruthless examiner, and no secular or spiritual judge can restore his easy sleep.
>
> By no means every conflict of duties, and perhaps not even a single one, is ever really "solved" though it may be argued over, weighed, and counterweighed till doomsday. Sooner or later the decision is simply there, the product, it would seem, of some kind of short-circuit. Practical life cannot be suspended in an everlasting contradiction. The opposites and the contradictions between them do not vanish, however, even when for a moment they yield before the impulse to action. They constantly threaten the unity of the personality, and entangle life again and again in their dichotomies.

> Insight into the dangers and the painfulness of such a state might well decide one to stay at home, … Those who do not have to leave father and mother are certainly safest with them. A good many persons, however, find themselves thrust out upon the road to "individuation". In no time at all they will become acquainted with the positive and negative aspects of human nature.'

As I read this, I knew that I was in the midst of an *individuation process*. Jung was explaining, to perfection, and in detail, the psychological trauma in which I had found myself. The knowledge that this condition of unresolvable inner conflict was a recognised process, a path trodden by others, brought me enormous relief. I was particularly struck by Jung's understanding, that this type of inner conflict must remain one's own. It is as if it has to be contained within oneself so that the opposites are constantly forced into contact with one another.

I am sure that, if you want to read it, you will find a great deal that interests you in this book.

Much love, Emilia

…

June 3, 1976

Dear Emilia

Your letter moved me deeply. I'm so glad that you found this explanation in Jung's writing. I think of Bapak's aphorism, *Experience first, explanations afterwards.* You certainly have had the experience of the inner conflict—and in full measure, and were ready for (and deserving of) an explanation. Who would say that it was not the will of God that you should get this explanation from another source of wisdom?

Your relief is my relief, just as your distress has been mine.

I will certainly get Jung's book and share what he has to say.

Love, Lamaan

Emilia's previous letters were always cheerful . Only now did she dwell on her inner conflict. She had perhaps, as Jung had said, felt compelled to keep it secret. I felt her distress and was very touched by her suffering. I knew about the failure of enterprises and I knew that some members were discouraged however, I had not been disturbed in the same way because I saw the setbacks as due to human failings, not a lack of guidance. Meantime, the subject of my letters had been about the outer impact of arriving back in a Western culture and my early encounters with the Subud group. My next letter showed that, although I had left Indonesia to make a new start, I still saw my life bound up with Subud activities.

June 11, 1976

Dear Emilia,

My impressions of Perth are very favourable. The people are friendly and the tempo of life is easy going. It appears prosperous, without ostentation. Of course my perceptions are bound to be comparative—after ten years in Jakarta! The feeling of the city is light. I mean that there is no heavy ambience—the daily struggle of life in Jakarta is a heavy emanation. You can feel it subside around 5.00 p.m. as the short twilight closes down the city. It is tangible, the collective relaxation of the daily stress of millions of people struggling to survive. Here the absence of this experience to which I had become accustomed—like a greater air pressure—makes me a little light headed. Emotionally I bounce along like a spaceman on the moon. Visually the city is modern and clean. The lamp posts are vertical, the kerbs unbroken, the lawn unworn. The suburban houses and their gardens are manicured, but the streets strangely deserted. It seems that even the wives and mothers go out to work each day. These are the simple contrasts to Jakarta.

I have started going to the latihan and have met most of the Subud group. There are about thirty men and women, several of whom I have known for many years from their visits to Cilandak.

Vernon Blakey was the Gurdjieff follower who told the ship's engineer, whom I met in 1954, about Ouspensky's books. I knew Vernon (then John) and his wife Hilda at Coombe Springs. Matthew Shanley, the engineer with whom I worked on the structural design for the S. Widjojo building, is here. There is a fair share of artists and teachers, mostly younger people, married couples and a few bachelors, all struggling to make their careers—film-makers, painters, and musicians. Keith Ewers, author of *With The Sun On My Back*, is the most successful.

I went along to the helpers' latihan and meeting last week. I had been looking forward to taking an active part in the helpers' work—expatriates in Cilandak did not participate in the organisation of the Centre. (We were not excluded, it was just that committee and helpers' work fell naturally to the Indonesians because of language). Although it is the normal practice, that helpers in Subud may be active wherever they are, I was told by one of the helpers that I should wait three months before participating in the meetings and testing. 'It is Bapak's ruling,' he said, 'It is a familiarisation period.'

I was angry—surprisingly angry, in fact! During the week, I was told that this ruling originated from one of the women helpers. 'She has control of the group's affairs,' my informant said, 'and her attitude has been a source of some discord amongst the members.' No doubt something in me felt personally frustrated, but perhaps I also had picked up the feelings of others.

Normally if there is a lack of consensus, the matter is referred to the helpers to test in the latihan and everyone abides by the outcome of testing. It seems that she will not agree to test—preferring to decide all issues from her interpretations of Bapak's talks. As consensus is essential, she effectively holds a veto.

Considering my reaction, maybe it's just as well that I do have a familiarisation period!

I hope this finds you well.

Love, L

...

June 22, 1976

Dear Emilia,

Today being Bapak's birthday, we had a party at the Subud House—trestle tables with white table clothes in the garden. There must have been almost forty of us with the children. Subud House is an old Federation style house with wide verandahs called *Brookside* on the Albany Highway, Maddington, about twenty minutes drive south from the city centre. It is on a large section screened from the road by trees and out of earshot of the neighbours —a quiet, very suitable location for latihan.

When I arrived in Perth, I found that the group had purchased a block of land in Wilson, closer to the city, with the intention of building a Subud hall. There was strong support in the group for the project and I was asked to join the building committee. I was full of enthusiasm and began by surveying the land. However in planning the site works I found that the section, which was near the river, would need so much filling—to raise it above the flood level—that development would be uneconomical. It would be cheaper to sell the land and buy elsewhere.

Meantime doing latihan in a number of small rooms in the house was unsatisfactory, so I suggested that we get the owner's permission to remove the interior walls and make the space into a hall. This sounds audacious, but the owner agreed, if we promised to put back the walls at the end of the lease. Everyone joined in the work. We installed a steel frame to support the ceiling so there was no need for columns. It went very well, except that I touched a live wire getting a electric shock which put me to bed for a few hours. With the whole space painted, carpetted and new curtains, the conversion is a very nice Subud hall at little cost.

I hope you are well.

Please write.

Love L

July 30, 1976

Dear Emilia

I'm working again. It became clear that it was going to be some time before land could be found for a new Subud hall, so I decided to take a job. Last week I signed a contract with a firm of consulting engineers to prepare a feasibility study for a new township for a gold mine. It suits me very well. I can use my experience of the INCO mining town in Sulawesi and at the same time become familiar with Australian building practices. An angel must have passed this way.

I've also become active in the helper's group.

Love, Lamaan

...

A week or so after I received Emilia's letter about her reading Jung's *Memories, Dreams and Reflections* I bought myself a copy. It was a memoir of Jung's lifelong exploration of his inner life and the psychology he developed from his work as a psychiatrist.

I found that, for Jung, psychology was not a theory, but an empirical science. He supported all his descriptions of the structure and function of the human *psyche* with clinical observations and the study of human history. At the same time, he was a spiritual man who respected religious experience. He saw the *psyche* as boundless and therefore in large part unknowable, hence mystical. He called the totality *the Self*, which he saw as comprising three broad realms: *consciousness, personal unconscious, and collective unconscious.* These we experience, he said, as: *the ego, the complexes (good and bad), and the archetypes of human behaviour,* respectively. Evidence of the existence of the *collective unconscious,* he showed, was to be found in the recurring symbolism of dreams and in the common themes found in the mythology of the world's people. He postulated the meaning of human existence as the unconscious psyche striving to become conscious of itself. (In *Memories, Dreams and Reflections* he describes this process as 'self-realisation of the unconscious.')

As a psychoanalyst Jung examined the interaction between our conscious and unconscious processes, but he went much further than analysis, evidencing that all creative activity, artistic and scientific derives from this interaction. The highest of these he saw as the development of the individual's potential wholeness, which he called *the individuation process.*

His description of *projection* as the way in which we attribute our own unconscious qualities onto others was for me one of his greatest spiritual insights. The withdrawal of our projections, on which individuation depends, is none other than the separation from our reactions central to, and made possible by, the latihan. *Individuation* was Jung's name for the spiritual or mystic path of true religion. He then went on, in his extensive writings, to identify the *archetypes* (imprints or patterns) met with in the process. In order of encounter: *the shadow*, (the rejected or undeveloped side), *the anima or animus* (the contra-sexual components), and others, leading ultimately to *the Self.*

When it came to religious experience, Jung continued to use his psychological language. He said that, 'In view of the clash of traditional symbols and psychological experiences ... instead of using the term God, (he would) use *unconscious,* instead of Christ *the Self,* instead of incarnation *integration of the unconscious,* instead of salvation or redemption *individuation,* instead of crucifixion or sacrifice on the Cross *realisation of wholeness.*' 'I think', he wrote, 'it is no disadvantage to religious tradition if we can see how far it coincides with psychological experience.'

Soon I began to see in Jung's writings events in my life as recognisable psychological happenings. Particular among these was the breakdown of a marriage resulting from a *mid-life crisis.* The overwhelming *anima* affects, he said, signalled a reversal of character to meet the needs of the second half of life. What I did not realise until later was that I was also undergoing a critical adjustment to meet the change from community life in Cilandak to solitary life in the West, an adjustment involving deep unconscious forces.

Meantime I found that Jung put great emphasis on dreams as the symbolic messages of unconscious activity. As a result I began to pay more attention to my dreams. I would write them down and try to interpret their meaning. My understanding of the imagery increased. It was fascinating. It was soon a kind of infatuation; I would spend my early morning hours engrossed in the interpretation of the symbolism. The more I attended to my dreams, the more dreams I had. On my own, without a busy social life, I was open to unconscious affects and did not recognise what was happening. Where Jung said we must respect the conscious viewpoint and maintain a balance with the unconscious, Sudarto once said: 'The inner world of dreams is an unbounded space. We are responsible to discriminate what is appropriate to follow in ordinary life.' I had allowed the dream world to be stronger, to encroach on my consciousness. In the weeks that followed I spent much of my spare time interpreting dreams, keeping a diary of explanations. For a time I was recording an average of three dreams a night.

I had been warned of the danger of being taken in this way by a dream I had had in Cilandak:

> I was in a room in the guesthouse which had a dividing screen of three panels made of woven raffia-type material. I walked around it and on the screen I could see a series of symbols or hieroglyphs. I realised that I could understand their meaning. Bapak was standing nearby and, seeing my obvious satisfaction in this newfound skill, he just smiled. His smile said, 'Don't be inflated, that's no big deal.'

I understood now that the screen was the barrier between the conscious and the unconscious. (In Indonesia these screens are used to divide off the sleeping space.) The symbols were dream images on the unconscious side. Bapak was a figure of higher wisdom who had cautioned me not to get caught up in this new ability.

The Ramadhan fast started on 25 August 1976, and as in recent years I followed it diligently, staying up until dawn most nights. On the twenty-first night I fell asleep in the early hours and dreamed:

When I did something to enjoy myself I became sad; when I tried to be comfortable I was uncomfortable—*everything I did had an opposite to the expected result.* The more I persisted, the less it was resolved.

It seemed to last forever until at last I awoke exhausted with an inner locution which pointed to a new balance between conscious and unconscious which had yet to be realised— *Dive not into the sea when you are called, but walk upon the shore and gaze into its depths.*

The dream showed me where my inquiries were taking me. I could now see that my work on dreams had become out of balance. I had gone 'behind the screen' (my Cilandak dream) and had become fascinated. I had forgotten Bapak's warning smile. Now the fasting had broken the spell.

I went out into the silent street and walked, seeking escape from the mind into my body. Gradually the winter darkness paled. Seldom had the light of dawn been so welcome.

During this inner excursion I had neglected my long-term needs. I had not tried to set up my own business, being content to earn only enough for my living expenses. For the past ten years in Indonesia I had found meaning in my work as part of the great unfolding of Subud activity near Bapak. In IDC I had also found fulfilment by being able to use my talent for organising work with other people. Now, without work in Subud and with an inner demand for new interests which were not yet clear I could find no enthusiasm for engineering. As a result a year after arrival in Perth, when offered a new contract with a mining company I felt that I could not go through with it.

In April I attended the Subud Australia National Congress in Sydney held at Pennant Hills hoping I might find a new opportunity to work with Subud members in Eastern Australia. Instead, on meeting old friends from New Zealand, I decided to visit them and see what was happening over there in Subud.

In Auckland I felt prompted to call on KRTA, the firm of architects and engineers, with whom I had worked in 1966 in Wellington. They now had projects in South East Asia and the Pacific and to my surprise offered me a job as a Public Relations Associate to produce their promotional literature. This seemed to be the change that I was looking for. I gave notice to my employer in Perth and moved to New Zealand. I was soon writing and engaging artists, photographers and printers—all activities of my feelings. It was also satisfying to be back at director level of a sizable firm and working with architects.

Once established in my work, I rented a house on the beach front in Howick, south Auckland, not far from Whitford where the Week family and other Subud families had recently settled. I had been a close friend of Mark and Istimah in Wisma Subud and now visited them regularly. Sandra their youngest daughter was ten at the time and I enjoyed being an 'uncle', helping with homework and reading books together.

I began attending the latihan in Auckland. It was a strong group of about one hundred men and women and had its own Subud House. I knew many of the members from earlier days and soon felt very much at home, joining in the helpers' work. This was to be the most active helpers' group I had known. We regularly tested questions for members and I learnt much that was valuable for my own understanding—sometimes from my mistakes.

One such mistake happened with a member with whom I had been testing questions for some weeks. During a general latihan I saw an image of him with disorganised office furniture in a latihan hall. I felt responsible to help him. As the image finished I heard the words 'Rose Cross'. When I told him my experience he became very excited and said that Rose Cross meant Rosicrucian. A week or so later I found that he had approached and joined the Rosicrucian Society. I was sure that this was not the correct interpretation of my receiving and regretted that I had not been more circumspect in talking about it.

Later I came to see that this kind of insight in the latihan carries with it a *feeling* from which we can decide what action, if any, to take, and that we have to stay in the latihan state until this *feeling* is quite clear. In this way we can understand what we have been shown. If the feeling is not clear we can make a wrong interpretation, as had happened with the Rose Cross = Rosicrucian assumption.

My experience with the member had been a statement of his condition, not an indication of an action that he or I should take. By doing latihan with him my inner feeling had recorded and revealed something about his problem. Until then, all I knew was that he was constantly questioning his life situation in terms of esoteric teachings, even his work and career. No sooner would we test one question than he would be back with another. The image in my latihan showed that something he was bringing to his worship, represented by the office furniture, was an obstacle to his latihan. I was trying to help him but couldn't (move the furniture). I continued to be puzzled about the meaning of Rose Cross. If Rose Cross did mean Rosicrucian, I thought, then the member must be doing something like a Rosicrucian.* I put it to him that his following of esoteric teachings may be an obstacle to his latihan.

The reader may ask if I am implying that the member's action in studying spiritual knowledge was an error. It is not a matter of judgement but rather of understanding the choices. Bapak was at that time travelling in Mexico and used a mythical story about two sons of Adam, *Sajid Anwar* and *Sajid Anwas,* to illustrate the difference between Subud and other spiritual groups which follow a way of study with the mind. He re-emphasised that the latihan kejiwaan of Subud is a receiving of the power of God.

* When I was writing this memoir I looked up a reference to the Rosicrucians. I found that the Rosicrucians had inherited their name from a movement which was expressed through the formula 'through the cross to the rose'. With it was an earlier alchemical drawing published in 1629 showing a rose growing out of a cross. The rose was shaped like a Subud symbol with seven layers of seven petals. The cross had a Christian meaning and the rose was described as an allegory of the seven stages of spiritual transformation. Applying this to the member, it appears probable that his preoccupation with esoteric teachings was his cross and this held him back from simply surrendering and following the transformation of the latihan.

You don't have to study, Bapak said, because the spiritual is in the hands of God. But it's up to you if you want to use your mind:

God is all-loving, God is all-giving to his creatures, so whatever man desires, whatever man hopes for, God gives him ... However, this latihan is not the way of Sajid Anwas [meditation or self denial], but is the way of Sajid Anwar [surrender to Almighty God].

Helpers in the Auckland group were very committed, both to serving the local members and to sharing their experience with helpers elsewhere. During 1977 our activity was extended to two nation-wide weekend meetings of men helpers, one in Wellington and one in Christchurch. Both went well.

When I heard that Bapak was attending the Australian National Congress in January 1978, I flew to Brisbane to meet him. I told him I had moved to New Zealand. He repeated his original advice, given to me in Indonesia, that I should return to Australia. This time he was more specific: 'Sydney or preferably Melbourne, but not that new place' (a group of members were newly developing land in Wollongong as a Subud centre). I felt that he had answered my unstated wish to be useful as possible to Subud.

~

Chapter Eight

Kejiwaan Councillor

In June 1978 I left Auckland and, after two weeks in Sydney and finding no immediate work possibilities, I moved to Melbourne. I had been living away from my home city for twenty-four years.

I soon felt settled. I attended latihan at the Heatherton Subud Centre and joined the helpers' group. It was a time when individuals worldwide were trying to follow Bapak's suggestion to start enterprises. I began looking for opportunities to work with other Subud members. Sinar Australia Pty Ltd had, with the encouragement of Sinar Enterprise Development in UK, just been incorporated as a trading company. I prepared a feasibility study for a small production plant to manufacture solar tiles for heating swimming pools. Most of those interested in the project were without business experience or capital and so it never proceeded. At this point, I had used up my capital and for the first time in my life I had to borrow money from my family. This period would have been more difficult had it not been for the fact that I was in Melbourne on Bapak's advice. As it turned out, I was approached soon afterwards by a large Australian firm of consulting engineers to prepare their company brochure. The work was extended to a series of capability publications—written project descriptions, illustrated with drawings and photographs. I began to travel to Brisbane, Sydney and Canberra for my client. Over twelve months I visited some hundred projects—highways, dams, bridges, coastal developments, environmental studies, etc. I set up a company and employed a graphic artist.

Through attending latihans in the cities that I visited and being an active helper in the Melbourne group, I got to know most of the Australian Subud membership in the eastern States. At the National Congress in Adelaide during the following Easter I was confirmed as a National Helper and tested to be the men's Kejiwaan Councillor (Spiritual Councillor) for Australia for the next four years.

The Councillors' term was from one World Congress to the next. This meant that I together with the women's Kejiwaan Councillor and the Committee Councillor for Australia were to attend the Subud World Congress in Toronto in August 1979 to get our briefing. Like many other members, I had always experienced a heightened state of wellbeing at Subud gatherings, particularly World Congresses, however my experience at Toronto stands out among the most special. Relationships were universally harmonious and sincere. I felt it was a glimpse of the understanding that the latihan could bring to mankind. I'm sure the fact that many of the almost two thousand attending were following the Ramadhan fast contributed to this feeling. A highlight for me came at the Idul Fitri *sungkum.** Bapak greeted me with surprise and joy, lightly touching my arm in a gesture of affection. I felt like a son receiving a blessing.

Bapak's testing of a member from Colombia in his last talk of the Congress made a strong impression on many I spoke with afterwards. Bapak had appointed several International Helpers and now showed us, by example, how they would fit into the helper organisation. After testing the talents of individual members from England and North America he asked if there was someone from South America. A man named Leonardo came forward. In reply to Bapak's questioning he said that he had just lost his job as an accountant. He was a very cheerful fellow and immediately had our sympathy. Bapak asked him to test and show his true talent, but he didn't receive a clear indication. Bapak then asked for a helper from Leonardo's home group to come up and test with him.

* Sungkum: Javanese gesture of respect to an elder performed at Idul Fitri (the end of the Ramadhan fast). It includes asking forgiveness for past mistakes.

The result was again unclear and Bapak now asked for a Regional or National helper. After some discussion someone was found but the testing remained inconclusive. Bapak then called one of the men who had been appointed as an International Helper. His testing was able to show that Leonardo would no longer be satisfied working as an accountant and that he would be better suited working with his hands as a mechanic. Bapak asked Leonardo if he felt he could find work in the technical field.

Leonardo didn't seem very confident. Bapak went on asking, 'What now? You can't leave a person in this situation. Subud Enterprise Services (SES) should now be asked to give some practical assistance. The two should work together, the helpers and the experts.' The incident was very moving. Not only did Bapak show us what to do, but he showed us by his example how to do it with the utmost concern, patience and perseverance. He was not content to finish the testing and discussion until an answer was found and Leonardo was genuinely satisfied.

Back in Australia the National Helpers Dewan (Council) set about organising a program of group visits. We were four pairs of men and women, representing the four regions of Australia. Our task was to support the local helpers. We lived great distances apart but had been allocated money by the membership to travel. Funds were sufficient for us to meet together as a full Dewan twice a year, each time in a different State, and travel in pairs of National Helpers within our regions at other times. This meant that in the Victoria-South Australia-Tasmania area we visited a group every six weeks.

When we met we had to adjust to working together as a Dewan. Even after we got to know and trust one another there were other lessons we had to learn before we became harmonious. One essential was to stay close to our latihan in everything we did—pausing frequently or stopping to do some latihan and testing. This was necessary because, in dealing with the problems brought to us, our feelings would become invaded by the force in the problem.

When this happened we would all talk too much, or disagree. We were passing the force on, causing disturbance and misunderstanding. Once we realised what was happening, we learned to restrain ourselves and hold the force inside until it *went to its right place.*

At other times our correspondence got at cross-purposes. The more we disagreed, the more the correspondence grew in volume and the more the problem grew. We were constantly being stretched, working at the edge of our capacity to go beyond our hearts and minds. Gradually we understood that the solution was to see our job, not as individual National Helpers with particular responsibilities, but as part of the National Dewan. We finally established a very close and loving relationship. Being a National Helper was an enormous privilege because of the understanding of human problems that it brought and for the inner blessing that the role carried.

We had our second National Dewan meeting in February 1980 at the Heatherton Centre. We had so many matters to discuss that had been referred to the Dewan that we were in danger of neglecting our contact with our host group. Fortunately someone realised this and we arranged to meet the members after the general latihans and test together. In the men's meeting this informal sharing paid off dramatically, resolving a number of personal problems.

A long-time member wrote in the Subud magazine *The Reporter*:

'The members of the National Dewan came with a "the-door's-open,-come-on-in" attitude that I had never seen before, and for which they have my admiration and my gratitude. The willingness with which the members rushed on in, and the results of this, were really astonishing. After all my years in Subud, I understood for the first time, this harmony of feeling that Bapak tells us is necessary for the growth of Subud.'

In those days there was strong financial support for helper and committee travel which meant that as Councillors we were able to to attend a national gathering of helpers in New Zealand in May.

This event strengthened the relationship between the two countries and led to a reciprocal visit by New Zealand National Helpers to Australia. It was also from this visit that we brought back the idea for holding a national gathering of helpers in Australia, such as had proved successful in New Zealand.

Throughout 1980 my work continued to require travel to all the Australian States except the Northern Territory. Wherever I went I took the opportunity to attend latihans and helpers meetings and so extended the contact of the National Helpers with the groups and the local helpers. This attention, like the earlier continuous travel around the country by the previous councillors, Leonard and Aisjah Parker, was much appreciated by the members, particularly in small groups, and contributed to a feeling of national brotherhood.

Early the next year I went as a Councillor to the First Subud Asian Zone Conference in Cilandak. It developed into an international event with the attendance of members of the World Subud Council, International Helpers, members of ISC, as well as the Councillors from fourteen South East Asian countries, a total of some hundred and fifty delegates and foreign observers. Bapak officially opened the *S. Widjojo* building and spoke of the great task facing Subud. He said the key to all achievement was harmony.

Bapak presided over the Conference plenary sessions. After the opening day the Councillors separated into Kejiwaan and Committee working groups where they discussed the issues active in each of the countries represented. It is difficult to describe the extraordinary love that grew between us as we each, of different cultures and religions, put the latihan into effect, speaking with respect and listening with patience, until we came to a consensus. At the closing session, a spokesman for each group reported to Bapak in the plenary session. On the Committee side Bapak said two things particularly pertinent to our enthusiasm:

Don't keep changing things or you'll make no progress.' And, *Don't get ahead of yourself with big plans for enterprise cooperation between countries. It is too early to expect much practical business interaction between countries in the Asian Zone.*

Bapak at the Subud Asian Zone Conference, Cilandak 1981
Photograph by Sahlan Cherpital

Bapak giving a talk in the S.Widjojo building Conference Room

The Subud bank, BSB, at the front entrance of the S.Widjojo building

Delegates at the Subud Asian Zone Conference, Cilandak 1981

Bapak and his wife Mastuti with delegates

On the Kejiwaan side, Bapak gave the memorable analogy: *The latihan is like a self-winding watch. You don't have to do anything to it. It just goes on working by itself, provided that you use it. But if you take it off and put it in a drawer, it stops.* He also gave a comprehensive explanation about the use of testing and introduced what was to become known as *body testing*—receiving (in the latihan) and allowing movements in each part of the body, one after another, until the whole body was moving, then adding the voice. He told us to take this back to our membership.

Bapak's final talk on19 January 1981 contained this passage: *Brothers and sisters, you need to understand something: If you want to be helped by people, you must also help people. If you want people to love you, you must also love people. And if you want people to cooperate with you and assist you, then you must also have that attitude towards them. This is what is called human justice.*

Now in facing our human life, we should understand that we have received the latihan kejiwaan from the power of Almighty God. So there is no lack or shortage of advice, teaching, instruction or guidance for us in our everyday lives and for our everyday needs.

Why is that? Because we have within us God's guidance and this guidance envelops our whole being inwardly and outwardly. And not only our own being but all of this created universe. God's knowledge and guidance are boundless and without boundaries. It encompasses the whole world and all God has made.

Bearing this in mind, brothers and sisters, why is it that you in Subud, still easily lose your way or come to the end of your tether, getting depressed with your life and your progress? How can this be when you have at your disposal the guidance of the power of Almighty God?

The duty of a Subud member is to create his own happiness. A Subud member may not in fact allow his life to sink into a state of disrepair, neglect or shortage. It is your duty as a Subud member to create that happiness, to create peace within yourself. Such is your responsibility to Almighty God.

Bapak takes the example of a bird. A bird when he leaves his nest in the morning can already sense which direction he has to fly in to find his livelihood, to find what he needs for food for himself and his family. It is as if he can already smell this before he leaves the nest. He senses where he has to go and what he has to do. Why then can't human beings be like the bird? Bapak doesn't say you have to be more than a bird. Bapak just means that you should be able to do at least like the bird does: You should be able to sense for yourself what direction you have to take for yourself in order for you to find your livelihood. That is the very least you should be able to do as a creature of Almighty God.

Bapak of course knows why you can't do that. The thing that stops you from ever reaching even the level of an animal is your own nafsu. The nafsu which is always worried. The nafsu which is always worried about what will happen if you do this or that, the nafsu that always wants something for nothing, that always wants to get as much as possible and give as little as possible. It is our tendency always to calculate to our own advantage. We always like to get as much money as possible for as little work as possible. We always like being helped but we try to avoid as much as possible having to help. On the other hand, we think to ourselves before we do something, 'Oh, if I do this, I'll fail.'

Don't precede everything you do with deciding what will happen afterwards. It is enough that you just follow. Follow what you receive or what you have to do within your life, your duty in your life. Then you will be given God's guidance. God provides man with everything he needs to fulfil his life in this world. God provides you with all the means of your livelihood each day of your life. That is why Bapak advises you: Don't put a curse on yourself through your own words.

Brothers and sisters, as Bapak has just told you, a Subud member is not allowed to let his life slide. It is his duty to form his own happiness, stability. But similarly, we are not allowed to let other people go short either. We are not allowed to have people around us who are poor or destitute. We have to help them. This is not only true of people who are in Subud but people who are outside of Subud as well. In order to do this, you have to be like Bapak: if you see a balance sheet, you only look at the expenditure. Like Bapak, you have to know that the income will come to fit this expenditure. If you want to be able to help others, you have to have that attitude. And for that attitude, you have to have a change of heart. You have to change your heart from a heart that worries, from a heart that's small, to a heart that is great.

A Subud member who has received the grace of Almighty God may not have a heart full of worries. You have to have a heart (such as termed in Javanese) that is as broad as the ocean. A heart that can truly contain the whole world. And this is something that, if you pray to God in Subud, you should pray for that thing. Pray to God to give you a heart as wide as the ocean. [Recording 81 CDK 3]

During the first quarter of 1981, I was able to travel to the groups in Sydney, Wollongong, Brisbane, and Adelaide to pass on what Bapak had shown us. *Zone One News,* published by the Zone Coordinators of the Asian Zone, did a splendid job in reporting the Conference, with full-length transcripts of Bapak's talks. *The National Reporter* also continued to perform well, communicating within Australia the sense of belonging to a Zonal neighbourhood which had developed at the Conference. This was a high point for Australia and the Zone.

At Easter the Subud National Congress was held in Brisbane. The National Dewan had decided to arrive four days before the Congress and prepare themselves by doing latihan and testing. Such was the close feeling of brotherhood with the Subud New Zealand National Helpers that, when invited, the whole of their National Dewan joined us, staying two weeks from 8 April to 21 April. A number of group helpers also arrived early. This was the first time Australian helpers had deliberately taken the step to prepare themselves in this way for a Congress.

The National Committee were invited and took part in the preparatory latihans. This arrangement meant that in effect the Congress started four days early, and in that time the participants had established a calm and quiet state in themselves. Instead of the first meetings of Congress being marked by long discussions and a sense of heavy business, it was easy, light and joyful.

Bapak's message to the Congress seemed like a confirmation: *...The right way is that you should preface anything you are going to discuss with your worship of God.*

About this time the timber house at the Subud Centre in Heatherton became vacant. I decided to move there and, because it was forty minutes drive from the centre of Melbourne, I would work from home. The Centre consisted of a hectare of land with two houses, one brick and one timber, and the latihan hall. Subud families lived in the brick house and in two neighbouring houses. I entered into an agreement to provide the capital to renovate the timber house and this was to be offset against the rent. I hired my niece, who was an architect, to remodel the house.

Living at the Subud House inevitably meant that members began to drop in with questions to discuss or test. My life was more than ever taken up with helper's work. It was a full and wonderfully rewarding time. Added to this I was to have the opportunity to visit groups in the Subud Asian Zone.

~

Chapter Nine

Visits to the Asian Zone

In May 1981 I began to travel to Thailand for my work. The project was a feasibility study for a fertiliser handling facility in Bangkok for the ACFT, the Thai Government Rice Cooperative. The funding came from the Australian Government Department of Trade and Resources. When I arrived bulk fertiliser was being imported through an existing wharf and warehouse on the lower reaches of the Chao Pyha River. Here peasant workers spent long hours in the dusty atmosphere hand-filling sacks and shouldering them on to barges for shipping up country. The study was to investigate the possibility of expanding and modernising the facility. I had an intense program of research, spending the days with local engineers, politicians and government officials, and the evenings writing up my findings. I also spent long periods at the existing fertiliser warehouses on the river collecting data to design a new wharf and bagging factory. It was important to choose a handling system that would increase the efficiency and throughput without reducing the labour force and one which would improve working conditions. This was done by introducing small conveyors for higher stacking and installing simple dust controlled bagging equipment.

It was my first visit to Thailand and I quickly came to appreciate the people's Buddhist attitude of tolerance and quiet acceptance of life. They were very nice people to work with. On the down side, the Thais are called the 'You-can't-do-anything-about-it-people.' The labourers working in the choking dust were an example of this and in Bangkok it was reflected in the chaotic traffic with its noise and pollution, and in the urban poverty and acceptance of prostitution.

There was a small Subud group in Bangkok which held latihan twice a week in the home of an Englishman, Kristiaan Inwood, married to a Thai. In one of these latihans I had a strong experience. I became deeply quiet and entered a state of extreme bliss. As I continued to surrender I saw inwardly, a short distance away, a statue of the Buddha sitting in the lotus position on a raised dais. My near surroundings were dark. The Buddha was translucent like green jade. I felt that the blissful state was connected with the image, as if I were experiencing a Buddhist state emanating from the Buddha. I noticed that the statue was lit from behind and I felt that the light from beyond the statue was the power of the latihan. My understanding was that the latihan was higher or more ultimate than the state of bliss. Along with this insight I was aware of a separation between the bliss and my inner self. The separation was tenuous. I did not want to give up the blissful state and leave it. The latihan lasted for about forty minutes and only when the helper called 'Stop!' did I gradually came out of it. I remained strongly affected, as one is in a state of love, for several days. This experience showed me the compelling attraction of Nirvana-like bliss and how I could easily wish to stay in that state. But I had also experienced that there was something beyond the bliss which was the goal of my surrender.

At the Subud Asian Zone Conference in January there had been some talk of helping Subud members to leave communist Vietnam. Most delegates had agreed that it was too dangerous for amateur intervention. At best, we could send them things they needed. When Ramdhan Simpson, who was the Australian Committee Councillor at the time, had said that he might go there I had tried to relieve the seriousness of his idea by quipping, 'When you come back, I'll have a cup of tea ready for you.' Now in a hotel room in Bangkok I welcomed Ramdhan. He had just come out of Vietnam. Normally he was a person who joked about everything. The Ramdhan I now met was badly shaken. We immediately did latihan. In my latihan I experienced utter despair. The suffering that Ramdhan had picked up I felt was unbearable. I don't know whether I felt the suffering of the members that he had met or the ugly ambience of the war-torn society, or both. When that was 'unloaded', he got his cup of tea.

The opportunity to travel in South East Asia fitted very well with the Kejiwaan Councillor role of fostering closer relationships within the Asian Zone. I was to return to Thailand three times and each time I extended my trip to visit other neighbouring countries.

The first of these visits was to Japan. This was a natural choice as Bapak had appointed the Japanese Councillors, Rozak Tatebe and Ichiki Toida as Zone Coordinators. We talked about their ideas for Australian cooperation with Zone publications and budget management. Almost immediately I arrived I felt myself following and participating in the nuances of Japanese manners and refined courtesy. This was the clearest experience that I had had of the potential of the latihan to allow us to enter into the character and behaviour of another culture. As a result I felt very much at home with my Japanese brothers and sisters. From their side the Tokyo group was most hospitable, providing accommodation in Subud House and delegating members to take care of my needs for a week, cooking meals and acting as travel guides. One, a professor's wife who spoke English, took me to the gardens near the Emperor's palace where, from the arch of a classic wooden footbridge, we watched golden carp swim in circles around our reflections and walked in a sea of purple irises bounded by aged and manicured pines. The men members worked long hours at their businesses, leaving home before dawn and returning after dark, yet some found time to take me to visit the Subud enterprises. DaishoTradingCompany was the most successful but there were several others, including one for building interiors, another for paper-making and a baby-minding creche. Outside the creche there was a neatly painted sign with what I thought was an incorrect Subud symbol. It had only four of the seven circles with seven rays. The family however explained that they had asked Bapak and he had given them this symbol for their enterprise. During an evening out at a restaurant I discovered another face of the Japanese—a night of almost continuous jokes and unbridled laughter. In Kyoto I was guided around huge timber temples and elegant gardens of sculptured trees thronged with tourists but wonderful to see. In Osaka I was accompanied to latihan down a maze of narrow lanes where I'm sure no foreigner was ever seen. The visit to Japan was in every way a most joyful experience.

On the way back to Bangkok I stopped over in Hong Kong, hoping to meet the group. Getting no reply from the contact numbers, I took a taxi to Husein Rofe's address. I found him at home and when I showed an interest in his translation services for my clients he enthusiastically showed me his new equipment for printing reports in foreign language characters. About Subud he explained that the group was fragmented and there were no regular latihan times, but he was able to give me the address of Nicky Carim, the Kejiwaan Councillor. It was late in the day before I was able to track Nicky down and then only to be told that everyone was too busy making money to be much interested in Subud Zonal matters or even to arrange a latihan with a visitor. 'Life is unashamedly materialistic,' he said. However we had latihan in his small apartment, and I departed for Bangkok the next morning.

A few years later Bapak's grand-daughter Indra said that Bapak had recommended that she and her husband Leonard not live for long in Hong Kong because of the strong effect of material forces.

In September I attended the National Congress in Christchurch with my fellow Councillors. In the evenings after latihan the men helpers conducted testing for individual members. The topics covered such important issues as finding the right type of work according to one's talent, becoming aware of personal blockages to spiritual progress, and for some, the direction of education for their children. Many people were helped. I took the opportunity to test with the helpers which countries in the Zone I should visit during my future travels. We received that Bangladesh was a high priority.

When the time came to go back to Thailand I decided to go via Jakarta and tell Bapak of my travel plans. Bapak asked about the situation in Australia and I was able to report on the recent close cooperation between the National Dewan and the National Committee. Bapak confirmed the value of such working together. 'It will help the Committee to avoid having doubts about their direction.' he said. 'And for the helpers it will avoid isolation of the spiritual from the material, which gives rise to problems of authority.'

He then cited as an example Sadat's confrontation with the fundamentalists of the Islamic clergy in Egypt, leading to his assassination. At the time the implication that I may have been divorcing the spiritual from the material at my personal peril passed over my head.

Bapak agreed about my going to Bangladesh and advised me to appoint more helpers and encourage the members.

After a week in Bangkok, working with a local economist on the ACFT feasibility study, I went to Dacca. I telephoned the Subud contact I had been given, Dr Mokaddem, who recommended a hotel near his home. It turned out to be a remnant of colonial times, spacious, high ceilings, tile floors, ceiling fans, and staff in white uniforms. It was a small oasis of cleanliness and quiet in a dusty and noisy city. He arrived an hour or so later and greeted me with a natural ebullience, speaking good English with charm and a ready smile. He explained that he was a medical doctor working for the government running a clinic several days a week, and went on to share with me the details of his life and plans. He was, he said, the only Subud member living in the city; the other three lived some hours away up country. He invited me to his home for the evening meal and left me to change. As I looked from my second floor balcony across the eastern landscape of low roof tops and mosque minarets, I remember feeling both the timelessness of the moment and strangely delighted with being here. Had I picked up these feelings from my new friend? I wondered. I left for his house in the growing dusk travelling in a battered taxi along dusty streets past broken plaster walls ancient with layers of faded posters and political graffiti. Most people walked and all were men in this strictly Islamic country. Mokaddem's wife served us a tasty meal of curried vegetables and other dishes, standing apart from the table and replenishing our plates, then joined us with her daughter for tea in the sitting room.

The next day I accompanied Mokaddem to his clinic. It was small and very simple in a poor and run-down district of the city—one room plus a bare waiting area—where the sick could come for free advice and basic treatment. I waited an hour or so while he attended to his patients, watching the passing scene on the worn and broken pavement outside. In a crowded minibus, he explained that he could leave the government and start his own practice but was continuing in the job because he felt useful. His happy demeanour and optimism confirmed he was at peace with his choice. We had lunch at the hotel and later did latihan in my room. Mokaddem hadn't been long in Subud and was grateful to share the latihan. I introduced him to testing, which was new to him. We tested to see the benefit to his country if more people could receive the latihan and, remembering what Bapak had advised about appointing more helpers, we tested how it would be for him to become a helper. He was reluctant to put himself forward but he did receive that he should approach his brothers and sisters, who were well-known people in Bangladesh, and tell them about the latihan.

It happened that the next evening one of Mokaddem's brothers was to have a family party. As a result of his receiving in the testing, he decided to go along and asked me to join him. Near the city centre we arrived at a large two-storey house set well back from a wide street. The cars parked in the driveway and the light streaming from the windows showed that the party had started. Mokaddem said that he didn't keep up with his family's social life, as his work and income were modest. Inside the well-appointed house I found a gathering of about thirty people including children, three generations of his extended family. I was introduced to an older brother, Mr G Kibria, Finance Secretary to the Parliament, and recently appointed to be Alternate Director of the World Bank for his region, and Mr Kibria's wife Nedera, a Professor of English at Dacca University. Nedera's sister, a heroine of the Bangladesh independence movement was there and a number of high-ranking army officers and other public figures. I felt the latihan flow strong in my body and feelings and, with some encouragement from Mokaddem, was soon answering questions about Subud.

The latihan brought a numinosity to the discussion which the people picked up and responded to enthusiastically, calling more of the adults from other parts of the house to come and hear about it.

The economist showed particular interest, asking about Subud in the USA. While I was talking I felt that something miraculous was happening. There I was in a state of latihan with people who were important to Bangladesh and I was telling them about Subud. I felt that this was an assignment from Bapak and carried a blessing.

Returning to Bangkok, I wrote to Livingston Dodson, a Subud friend in the USA, asking him if he could follow up the contact with the World Bank economist in Washington. As for the others I had met at the party, I could only report to Bapak what had happened and leave it to the Zone Coordinators to follow up.

Mokaddem confirmed the benefit of the visit for him and he remained an active member of Subud thereafter.

Back in Australia, Halimah Armytage and I as National Helpers for the South East Region visited Adelaide and Hobart. In Adelaide we were welcomed with enthusiasm and joyful feelings but soon found there was some tension in the men's group. The problem was that an older man was disturbed in the latihan by the noise made by a younger member. The latter in turn felt he should have the freedom to be noisy. They were irreconcilable on this issue. At first it seemed obvious enough that the older man should be more patient and try to surrender his feeling of disturbance. However, when I did latihan with them I received that there was more to it. The older man's desire for quietness was a kind of rigidity limiting his surrender and the younger man was adding to his already very active latihan additional sounds which did not come from his latihan. While both reacted to the other they remained unaware of their own manifestations. Armed with this understanding I tested with each of them. Unfortunately neither could separate from his reactions to the other enough to see his own situation. It was not a problem that could be solved in one short visit.

In Hobart we found that attendance at the men's latihan had been falling off and the helper had become rather discouraged. All the members turned out for our visit and there was talk of moving the latihan from the present small rooms to a larger venue.

I suggested instead that they enlarge the two rooms into a small hall by knocking out the dividing wall. They obtained permission from the owner and we did the work ourselves, making the occasion an opportunity for remembering our latihan as we worked. The benefit of these three days together revitalised the men's group.

In November the Dewan of National Helpers met in Perth. It was for the first time in four years. The National Committee Chairman and the Committee Councillor decided to visit at the same time. As Bapak had suggested a few weeks earlier, we had brought the helper and committee activities together. The visit was a great success. For the committee it was an opportunity to involve the Perth members in the discussions then under way in Australia about an International Subud Centre in Sydney. For the helpers we achieved more than we could have hoped for. We were given a house for conducting interviews and for four days met continuously, daytime and evenings, testing individually with members who, through their isolation, were stuck in some aspect of their Subud or private life. We were also able to break a long deadlock in the helpers' group and confirm the appointment of new candidate helpers.

It was during this visit that I had an experience in the latihan where my inner feeling was used to help someone without my initiative or direction. It was in the group latihan. I suddenly started to weep and felt a terrible grief. I continued to surrender until it finally lifted, leaving me feeling deeply cleansed. I knew that it was connected with one of the members. After the latihan the member came to me and said that he felt a great burden had been lifted from him in the latihan. He said that some weeks before he had allowed his baby daughter to play near some wire in his factory where she had damaged one of her eyes. He blamed himself for the accident and could not escape the despair. I understood that through the latihan I had, entirely without my conscious intention, experienced and surrendered the grief and despair which the member could not surrender for himself.

I returned to Thailand for the third time in December and took the opportunity to travel on to India and Sri Lanka. There had been few overseas visitors to India since Bapak's last world journey in 1970 and it was clear, when the Indian Kejiwaan Councillors had failed to attend the Asian Zone Conference, that there was a need for someone to go there and see what help could be given. The Asian Zone Coordinators, who themselves were not free to travel, warmly supported any visit. I contacted the Indian Councillors and they suggested that I go to the three main groups, Calcutta, Bombay, and Madras, and in this way see as many members as possible. I arranged to stay two days in each place and two days in Colombo.

I flew from Bangkok to Calcutta. I found the conditions for the people of the city worse than I could have imagined. Devastation had been added to the desperate poverty and neglect that was endemic. Long stretches of the main streets in the city centre had been excavated for a subway and left to lie open for lack of funds.

In Subud I found that there were only ten active members and one remaining helper, where a few years before there had been several hundred. I was asked on my arrival to visit and do latihan with a dying member, lying gaunt and wasted on a rope stretcher. Strangely, this latihan was a turning point for me. Where my initial reaction to all this wretchedness had cut me off, I now felt myself belonging in that moment, in that place, close to these people and their situation. From the dying man's house we went to collect a long-time member who, I was told, had not done latihan for some time. We were asked to come in and wait. A few minutes later a holy man with robes and long hair appeared from inside the house and departed through the front door without a word. Soon after, the member came out from the same place. From his flustered welcome I realised he was embarrassed because we had interrupted him with his guru. We crowded into an ancient taxi and arrived at the house where latihan was to be held just as rain began to fall. After the latihan I gave the latest Subud news about the developing activity in our Zone. It seemed to touch a chord in their feelings.

They had known better days in Subud, when there had been a flourishing group, and they had looked to the latihan as the promise for a better life. They began to talk with enthusiasm about the inactive helpers coming back. It was a lesson in hope.

As the evening went on I could hear the wind and heavy rain beating down outside. We had been on the edge of a cyclone in the Bay of Bengal and now it had arrived. By midnight the electricity had failed and objects could be heard crashing around the house. There was no chance of getting a taxi, so my host said he would walk with me to my hotel about a kilometre away. Outside, the howling wind, loaded with solid sheets of rain, battered every moving thing. The noise was deafening. Loose shutters banged and clattered, walls and buildings seemed to scream, trying to escape the relentless gale. Flashes of lightning lit the total blackness of the night. I glimpsed trees and branches fallen across the road, which had become a river of swirling water, its surface whipped into a frenzy. I had come out with my umbrella up but it was blown inside out. In a moment I was drenched. All I could do was follow the dancing torchlight of my friend. By the time we got to the main street two blocks away the water was above my knees. As the water became deeper the spray was blinding. I wondered where the open manholes might be and thought I might be swallowed up. I tried not to lose my friend, now well ahead, a small silhouette in a lightning flash.

My mind was suddenly clear and still. The latihan was strong. I felt at one with the dramatic surroundings. *Alone in a dark flooded street in Calcutta in a cyclone*. Rising water. Lashing rain on my face. The roar of the storm. I thanked God and pressed on against the wind and water.

Half an hour after leaving the house we arrived on the steps of the hotel. My brother turned back without a word and disappeared into the darkness. I pulled off my shoes, adding to the pool of water on the smooth marble floor of the brightly-lit foyer.

My next visit was Bombay. I wrote at the time:

'Manavendra Bose, the Committee Councillor for Subud India, met me at the Bombay airport. Looking well and prosperous, he greeted me with his warm and humorous smile and took me to his comfortable apartment. His wife Hasiyah is from a Bangladesh family and has the characteristic interests of her people in the arts—which has made them the poets and writers of the sub-continent. They were the perfect hosts, treating me to lunch at one of Bombay's new luxury hotels and taking me to see the new and fashionable high-rise developments near the ocean. The weather was balmy.'

After my experience in Calcutta the contrast could not have been more extreme. It was as if, through providence, I should see the two sides of India—the poverty and the affluence.

Membership of Subud in Bombay had never been large but now it had almost totally dispersed. Some, I heard, had re-established a Khrisnamurti group. In spite of this my hosts spoke with hope of reinvigorating Subud throughout India. Manavendra and I did latihan and tested about what he could do. It was clear that he would have to have a much stronger intention if anything significant was to happen. Hasiyah was the Indian Kejiwaan Councillor for the women. I told her about the two women probationers waiting to be opened in Bangladesh. She agreed she would go there if funds could be found. Later in Australia I was able to arrange her travel costs.

After two days I flew to Madras in the south of the country. The Madras and nearby Bangalore groups were the most active in India at the time. I was met by Maitreya, the Indian Kejiwaan Councillor for the men. Devoted to the latihan, he was the local helper and elder figure to a dozen or so young men who made up the local group. That evening we did latihan in the open on the flat roof of one of their houses. Miraculously, the sounds of their vigorous latihan vanished into the night air and surrounding coconut palms without seeming to disturb or draw the attention of neighbours. Afterwards we sipped tea together under the stars as they enthusiastically plied me with questions about Subud.

They were mostly young bachelors, well educated, but poor. I found out later that they spent most of their meagre incomes on charitable works in the community.

Maitreya and I met several times at my hotel for latihan. Our testing showed how important it was for Subud in India that he travel to visit other groups and, on the question of funding, that he should accept financial help from the Zone—although accepting charity was against his principles. He confided that he had felt isolated and was particularly grateful for the opportunity to do testing with another helper. For me, sharing worship with this good man alone justified my trip to India.

Established in 1957, Colombo was one of the first Subud groups outside Indonesia. When I visited there were about fifty active members and they had long owned their Subud House. The group, I found, had been for many years almost completely isolated from contact with other Subud members because of the country's political situation, which made foreign travel impossible. After the latihan the ladies had arranged a supper but before it was served I was asked to answer any questions. Whereas in Madras the members were relatively new and needed to confirm their latihan experience with a visiting helper, here in Colombo the situation was quite the opposite. Most members had been in Subud since the early days and all but three of the twenty men were helpers.The questions centred on the responsibility of helpers to expand the membership. Speakers expressed their opinions rather dogmatically, as if, I thought, to provoke the views of others without exposing their personal doubts on the issue. Someone asked about testing. Here my examples of questions that we had tested in New Zealand—where we spontaneously followed the needs of the situation in framing our questions—brought an explosion of debate. Some said that this approach validated their long-withheld feeling that everyone should be free to follow their own receiving. Others disagreed. Having gone through disappointing experiences where rapid growth in membership had not been sustained, they insisted that there would be problems unless questions were prepared before testing began.

It seemed from the passion of these discussions that a lot of energy was being suppressed by the prevailing dogmatism. Some wanted to test; others resisted. Nothing happened. Instead question time ended and we retired to a banquet-sized supper. Later I realised that this propensity for vigorous debate was what made some Ceylon people such excellent public speakers. I passed on all this to the Zone Coordinators and the International Helpers whose job was to travel regularly to isolated groups to help with such questions.

Throughout the visit my hosts were extremely hospitable, entertaining me to dinner and showing me the sights. As I was driven through the city I recognised several faded buildings that I had seen in their colonial splendour thirty years earlier. Colombo like its people was caught in a time warp. After two days at Subud House I returned to Bangkok. This was the last of my business trips to Thailand and the last of my opportunities to visit Subud groups in Asian Zone countries. I travelled from there to Auckland.

Bapak's world tour that year had been reported regularly in Subud World News. Now, talking to Erling (Mark) Week, who had travelled with Bapak in North America in June and July 1981, he fired my interest to get a copy of Bapak's talks of the journey, published as *All of Mankind.*

I was particularly interested to read Bapak's insightful explanation of the problem of *I* as encountered through the inner process of the latihan—the problem of *I* that had sparked my interest in the inner life at Coombe Springs twenty-five years earlier. I read:

... Bapak wants to explain to you about the word 'I'. The word 'I' is a very important thing to have and use. But if you misunderstand it or misuse it, or if you are not clear about it, then it can also be very dangerous, because we say all the time, 'I do this' or 'I do that' or 'I know that.' But who is 'I'?

The nature of a human being embraces what we call the lower forces. These are elements of life in this world which participate in our being and through which we are able to live here. They start with the material force. If we were oblivious to this force we would be unable to create our houses, clothes, transport and so on.

There is the vegetable life force, which we get from eating and so makes up our physical body, and the animal force which comes to us through the meat and microscopic organisms.

Then there is the life force of human beings. All these and higher forces co-inhabit our being. These are our friends. So we have to be aware of them, and we have to live with them and know how to deal with them. If we really knew it, God has been incredibly wise, kind and perfect in what he has created for us in this world. But these life forces are only for this world. They accompany us only to the threshold of death, because beyond that we no longer need them and we no longer can share our life with them.

To repeat, our being is filled with life forces, each of which is vying for influence within our being. [We feel them as our needs, wishes and desires.] So when we say 'I', it's not at all easy to be clear who is 'I' and who is influencing 'I' at that moment.

The purpose and significance of the latihan kejiwaan is to enable us to experience the separation of 'I' from all the lower forces which manifest within us through the nafsu (passions). The latihan trains us to constantly experience the separation of 'I', or our real 'I', from all these lower forces so that gradually we get to know who is 'I' when 'I' is no longer influenced by the material, vegetable, animal and the human.

[Recording 81 YVR 1]

CG Jung describes the same dilemma in psychological terms in his *Collected Works 11*, pars 138-49: 'We have got accustomed to saying ... "I have such a desire or habit or feeling of resentment," instead of the more veracious "Such and such a desire or habit or feeling of resentment *has me.*"'

Mary Watkins in referring to Gurdjieff's claim that we spend most of our lives in a state of waking sleep also puts it clearly in her book *Waking Dreams*, 1971: 'As our thoughts, feelings, and actions come to the edge of our conscious field, our awareness goes out to meet them and merges with them. As our awareness becomes absorbed and attached to the emotion, thought or action, *we become it.*'

The year 1981 saw Subud activity in Australia and the Asian Zone expanding rapidly. A growing closeness between members in different countries in the Zone was reflected in the publishing of *The Reporter* as a joint Australian and New Zealand magazine and the launching of *Zone One News* with Japan. Although we didn't know it at the time, this enthusiasm and show of capability was a prelude to the coming of the International Subud Committee to Australia, and the attempt to build an International Centre in Sydney.

So much was happening in Australia which required policy decisions from the members it was decided to call an Australian Compact Congress in Sydney at the end of January 1982, instead of waiting for the next bi-annual National Congress in 1983. The National Helpers Dewan would meet at the same time.

It was an extremely busy occasion. The National Committee had its agenda of business to complete with the group delegates; the Sydney group members expected time with the National Helpers; and the International Centre Project team wanted to use the occasion to present their progress report—all in three days. In addition we were joined by the New Zealand National Helpers, swelling our Dewan meeting to fourteen men and women.

Soon after arrival matters became complicated when the National Helpers were asked to resolve a problem in the Sydney helpers' group. It transpired that prior to Congress one of the older men helpers had unilaterally appointed several members as candidate helpers. Several of the other Sydney helpers and a majority of members did not agree with these appointments. Because of the seriousness of the difficulty and to increase the chance of us receiving the right answer in our testing, we asked the New Zealand National Helpers to join us in the testing. This meant we were seven men National Helpers and seven or so Sydney men helpers. First we had a latihan together with the proposed candidate helpers. Then we tested with each candidate separately, asking him to show his suitability to become a helper at that time. The receiving of the National Helpers was unanimous that three of the candidates were unsuitable. The older helper who had appointed them disagreed and insisted that he had received otherwise. He would not accept the testing.

The candidates agreed to follow the testing and withdraw but the older helper was for a time upset with us, and with me in particular because as Kejiwaan Councillor I had been spokesman on behalf of the Dewan.

Apart from that one incident the Compact Congress went very well. On the Saturday night the men's latihan was crowded with about fifty members. As it finished we tested together—receiving the latihan in parts of the body in the way Bapak had suggested at the Asian Conference. It was dramatic. Almost everyone responded with vigour. It was the first time I had tried testing with a group and I only did so with such a large number because it felt right at the moment. (Normally we did this testing with individuals or small numbers). Several people came up afterwards and said that they had greatly benefited from the experience. Two or three had to be told to stop because it was overwhelming.

In April 1982 Bapak began a two-month Asian tour, coming to Australia, New Zealand and Japan, and arriving in Sydney on 8 May. The Melbourne group made a big effort to prepare for the visit. The brick house was extended and the new wing furnished for Bapak, the latihan hall was redecorated, and garden paths paved. The car park was also completed and a marquee erected in the grounds as a dining hall for visitors. The timber house was used as a centre for helper activity. Bapak stayed ten days.

When it came to his four talks to the group—Bapak emphasised the need for helpers to care more for the members. He seemed disappointed with their progress. He then tested some of the helpers and National Helpers. I particularly remember three of us being moved to show the walk of army generals of various nationalities. This type of testing served to show that the latihan developed our capacity to know the character of people. These talks were recorded on video tape. (Melbourne, 7 May 1982)

Bapak had started his visit in Perth and had been joined by a number of overseas visitors. Among them was a group of about ten South African members who had taken the opportunity to see Bapak in Australia because they could not get visas to enter Indonesia.

When they arrived in Melbourne they asked Bapak for an interview. The meeting was held in the sitting room of the timber house and may not have been recorded. Bapak was asked, 'How can we attract the black people of our country to the latihan?' He said:

If you go to them and try and encourage them to join, they will be nervous of you and your intentions. They will certainly not be comfortable to join you. But if you really want them to join, then they will feel the sincerity of your attitude and will feel free to come. It is a matter of attitude.

A number of us travelled to Sydney where Bapak confirmed that the next ISC, starting 1983, would be in Australia. Then, with an ever-enlarging party, we continued on to New Zealand for Bapak's ten-day stay in Auckland. He arrived in mid-May and moved into Mark Week's beautiful house in Whitford. The party consisted of Bapak and Mastuti, Rahayu, Muti, Tuti and Sjarif. No expense was spared in preparing for and taking care of them. A large part of the New Zealand membership attended Bapak's talks and a school hall was hired for latihans. As the visit progressed he conducted a series of tests in front of the members—to choose a new committee, to illustrate the action of forces in our lives, and to show individuals traits in their nature.

One of these sessions was particularly important for me. In testing me he revealed *a priest* in my character. The test clearly showed that I was not balancing my outer and inner life. This had a very strong impact and I resolved to redress this inbalance by turning my attention more actively to my professional work.

Some time later I recalled an experience that I had in the first years of latihan at Coombe Springs in which I rejected my maternal grandfather. The experience had always puzzled me because he was the most religious person in my family line—a Baptist lay-preacher who had lived an exemplary Christian life to the end of his days. Now I saw that what I had received to reject was not my grandfather *per se*, but a propensity that I had inherited, or learned in childhood, to live like a *priest* in outer life.

After the Idul Fitri celebration at the end of July I visited Central Kalimantan with a small group of members, which included Harlinah Longcroft, Sahlan North, Simon Gerrand and Hassan Vogel, to see the site for the proposed Subud township at Tengkiling. We flew from Jakarta to the southern port city of Banjamasing and then travelled by speedboat up the huge rivers of the southern delta. It took six hours to reach the inland provincial capital of Palangka Raya. From there we were driven along an old Russian road to the village of Tengkiling. It was a joyful trip, the more so because we had just completed the Ramadhan fast. I felt a great sense of optimism. Here was a virgin place free of constraints. At the village of Tengkiling I immediately saw from the high water marks on the houses that the Subud land was susceptible to flooding. I hired survey equipment from the government offices in Palangka Raya and examined the river level records. My measurements established that about one-third of the land we had bought was regularly flooded and was therefore unsuitable for housing development. I wrote a detailed report for the Subud Kalimantan Committee who, as a result, began to negotiate for additional higher land.

Back in Australia, Sharif Horthy called me from Jakarta asking me to bid for the engineering design of Bapak's hotel project. This was a proposal for the S.Widjojo company to build a large modern hotel in Jakarta. An architectural concept had been developed by Hassan Vogel and preliminary feasibility studies had been produced. I contacted Mathew Shanley, with whom I had worked on the S.Widjojo building design, and Warnock & Chapman one of Sydney's best structural engineering consultants. We prepared a joint-venture offer detailing the complete design and drawing schedule with manhours and costs. It was used as a comparison with an offer by the Hong Kong branch of the international consultants Ove Arup & Partners who designed the engineering of the Sydney Opera House. The hotel project did not proceed because the cost of other large scale Subud projects was stretching the investment capacity of the Subud membership.

Meantime I continued to travel as a National Helper to the main centres in Australia, then in November flew to New Zealand to attend a men helpers' gathering in Wellington. These nationwide gatherings had been held three times a year since 1976 and attracted twenty or so active New Zealand men helpers. Helpers need experience if they are to assist members with testing questions and the intent of these gatherings was to widen the helpers' experience through extended periods of latihan and testing over three days. There was no agenda. The latihan produced the topics for testing. There was, however, a conscious decision to avoid hypothetical problems and deal only with real situations. This meant that the helpers' own personal questions were as much the topic of tests as were the unsolved problems they brought from their groups. A feature of the meetings was the testing with the candidate helpers present to find their strengths and weaknesses. Clearly they gained confidence by this experience and their attendance at the gathering did much to forge a good working relationship with the older helpers. Later this experience was shared with the helpers in groups around Australia.

~

Chapter Ten

International Subud Centre

In April 1982 we heard that Bapak had a special receiving in Perth which indicated that Australia should be one of five locations in the world for an International Subud Centre. These Centres are physical facilities with a latihan hall, resident helpers and a secretariat where the worldwide spiritual and organisational activities of Subud are administered. The first was *Wisma Subud* in Indonesia which had a large residential component, and the second was *Anugraha* in England, a conference centre being built at the time.

When Bapak arrived in Sydney he launched the Australian International Centre project and gave it the name Susila Dharma. (Later this was changed to Project Sunrise.) He selected five directors through testing, Ramdhan Simpson, Joshua Baker, Luqman Keele, Livingstone Armytage and myself. Whereas Bapak had personally directed all previous international projects—Cilandak, the S.Widjojo Centre, the BSB Bank, Anugraha and the Jakarta Hotel, he now indicated that the Australian International Centre would be up to us. Sydney was confirmed as the location. With the coincidence of the Subud World Congress with the Australian Bicentenary in 1988, Subud's interest focussed on Darling Harbour where the Sydney City Council had proposed an extensive re-development of the railway yards into a multi-purpose public and commercial facility to celebrate the event. The decision on the project was to be made by the New South Wales State Government. Our idea was that Subud might build a conference centre along the lines of Anugraha as part of the re-development.

I started with goodwill towards Luqman. I hadn't worked with him before, but I felt that he would bring an expansive and visionary approach to the work. He was creative, talented and very hard working. He assumed the leadership role. Under his direction the scope of the Susila Dharma project rapidly expanded into an assessment of the re-development plan for all of Darling Harbour. To an extent this was justified. Any opportunity that Subud might have depended on the government developing the whole site.

On 3 July 1982 at the end of Ramadhan, after presentation of a concept plan to the Premier of New South Wales, Neville Wran, the Susila Dharma team travelled to Indonesia to report to Bapak. About the meeting with the government he said, 'Bapak feels that we are going to meet with thorns along the way. ...' 'Thorns' were not a 'brick wall', so we assumed we should persevere.

On 7 January 1983 I moved to Sydney to work fulltime on the project. Apart from director's duties concerned with company matters, property purchases, and so on, I prepared a number of engineering studies—the excavation of the harbour to its original shoreline; the repair of Pyrmont Bridge (support from the Institution of Engineers Australia, contributed to its being saved from demolition); and traffic patterns and parking requirements for the Pyrmont peninsula. I also worked with quantity surveyors to produce construction programs and cost estimates for various schemes.

The scope of the project continued to expand and with it the costs of the studies. At the personality level it wasn't long before there were difficulties. The board of directors would meet and agree a budget only to find at the following meeting that the company had been committed to new expenditures beyond its resources by Luqman. Borrowings began to soar. The other directors became concerned and some of us alarmed. The problem was taken to Bapak. He suggested that the consultants (architects, engineers, planners, designers, etc) be set up as a separate entity to the holding (finance) company. He referred to the Anugraha project, where the architect was in the holding company and things were also not going well financially for the same reason. Bapak gave the consulting entity the name *Budhi Susila*.

This separation of responsibility had always been the most common form of organisational structure for development projects worldwide. It provides the necessary checks and balances between finance and design which make projects economically feasible. The importance of this advice, however, was not appreciated and Bapak's guidance was not implemented. In my view this was the turning point for the project. From there on there was no accountability. We began to 'reap the whirlwind'.

As time went on another problem developed. This was a loss of direction. Bapak had given us the task of producing an International Subud Centre, a building. This required an architect's professional methodology starting with an assessment of Subud's needs and production of a clear brief. Luqman had no architectural training or knowledge. He was a filmmaker. As I saw it, he treated the project like a film story; it wasn't grounded in material reality. Bapak tried to solve this by advising him to study architecture. In spite of his willingness to study, there was of course not time to master the disciplines of building science. And the fact that the team did not have a clear brief for the International Subud Centre building meant that every time a practical difficulty arose, such as our siting of a Subud facility on public or prohibitively expensive land, the project was redefined. At one stage the International Subud Centre project was changed from a building to a consulting enterprise. After a time this way of working became a headlong rush from scheme to scheme, hoping to strike the right answer. Bapak said, 'Luqman has too many ideas' and tried to help the situation by appointing an American geologist as managing director. This didn't solve the problem. Although the responsibility for administration was separated from the design function the lack of clear direction continued as before.

By July I had become very dissatisfied with the situation. I several times sought guidance through testing as to whether to resign. The receiving was that I should not.

...

During this period, from 13 to 22 March 1983, I attended the Asian Zone Congress in Jakarta. At that time congresses made up of Councillors were the point of distillation of World Subud experience. It was still possible for Councillors through their dewans and committees to know what was happening within the membership and so truly to represent them. Although Compact Councils and International Helper meetings later took over this role, I remain convinced that the original Councillor structure produced the most effective exchange of real experiences. The (later) upper layer tended to lose touch with the membership.

The Conference was described as: 'The long-awaited forum for Councillors to discuss overall trends in Subud life and the chance to check and compare progress in each others' situations and circumstances.' It was a most harmonious and productive time. The Kejiwaan Councillor meetings were conducted with such respect for the latihan and each other that it was a joy to participate. There was a variety of opinions about the use of body testing. A concise report on the topics discussed was submitted to Bapak with questions, one of which was: 'To what extent should helpers practise body testing with the members to feel the latihan in all parts of the body?'

Bapak responded with a long talk. He said, 'To answer your question, Bapak wants to start by explaining to you that in tackling a problem we have to approach it comprehensively and not piecemeal.' This made a lot of sense to me. I felt he was saying that we should try to understand the principle instead of looking for a ruling.

A theme of Bapak's talks was the results of the latihan. 'Subud is based on proof,' he said. He asked us for examples of the benefit of the latihan in our lives. He went on to say how everything has its consequences. Even birth deformities of children (which often seem so unjust) were a consequence of something. *The Zone Reporter* brought out a special issue which gave an excellent coverage of the proceedings and SPI published Bapak's talks in the colour magazine *Subud World.*

Two weeks later in Australia the spirit of cooperation enjoyed at the Asian Zone Conference became a cornerstone of our National Congress in Melbourne. The needs of the other countries in the Zone became our needs and Bapak's explanations to the Kejiwaan Councillors became the starting point for a fresh look at helpers' work. The Zonal Conference was achieving real results.

As the World Congress at Anugraha in England approached, I decided I would visit Muchtar Martins in Portugal. I had known him in Sydney during his work as an architect on Project Sunrise and was interested to know more about his current plans for a Subud development at Albergaria, Bucelas. At least that was my intention. I arrived in London on 24 July 1983 and immediately took the ferry to France and the train through Spain to Lisbon. From the moment I boarded the cross-Channel ferry my attention was drawn to the young people going on holiday. I was shocked by their rough behaviour. Their language and movements were coarse and they acted without consideration for anyone or anything. It was more than the exuberance of youth, there was something wild and barbaric about them. I was dismayed and sad—this was the next generation whom I would rather have loved and respected. On the train in France the European students were much the same.

Muchtar kindly, and at some inconvenience, put me up in his flat for a four-day stay. What I didn't know was that I had arrived at the same time as the Subud Youth Camp was being held at Albergaria. I went out to the site and found it attended by a large colourful group of young people from many countries. I had a good impression of their demeanour compared with those I had encountered on the ferry. As time went on I found that there was a wide range of ages and backgrounds, and this meant that younger children from more conservative backgrounds were brought together with older youth from more permissive cultures. Parents had allowed their children to attend on the understanding that it was a supervised Subud camp. In fact there were too few adults to set and maintain the ground rules. Soon I heard that there were problems with minors drinking alcohol in the local village.

Muchtar Martins and guitars at Albergaria Youth Camp 1983

Subud Youth entertain themselves with music and outdoor theatre

The adults in charge seemed to be caught unprepared. I stayed much of my time at the camp as it gradually settled down and became more creative, with music and theatre.

Looking back, I believe my reaction to the state of the young people on the boat and train was an intuition of the potential danger at the youth camp. In fact my whole trip's value, if any, was to be another adult presence at Albergaria during those few days. The responsibility of parents for the supervision of their children was confirmed by Bapak two weeks later in his talk to the Subud young people at a special session of the World Congress. In a moving talk Bapak described the importance of the young for the future of Subud. This is an excerpt:

Brothers and sisters it is really very important for human beings, and that includes all of you, to understand the history of mankind in this world and the background to our lives here as human beings. Of the equipment that God has given to man, the most important part is that which is within his own being; that is, his physical body, his faculties and his heart and mind. The heart and mind will work and will operate in this world providing they are accompanied by and fuelled by the lower life forces ... that is, the material, the vegetable, the animal and the human.

It starts with the influence of the material. When a child is very young, he loves to have toys to play with. And also he cannot cooperate with other children. If children of that age are together they must quarrel. It's part of their nature. All they are interested in is having a toy. They are just happy to grab it. So, whatever it is, they will grab it. If it's a knife, they will grab it and cut themselves.

So that's the function of the parents. It's the parent's fault if he gives them a knife at that age. It's the parent's responsibility only to give them things that cannot hurt them and that help them to develop.

The first influence on a child is material things, but then gradually we come to the influence of the plant world or the vegetable world. That is when children suddenly become interested in eating and they eat an enormous amount; and they just want to eat and eat, so people say they eat like buffalos but their work is not as beneficial as buffalos because they are not yet able to translate all that food into useful work. But eating is good for them because at that moment their bodies need to grow and this wish to eat is necessary. But it also signifies the influence of the vegetable forces upon their being.

Then at a certain age children come to the point when the animal forces begin to influence them. And this is the moment when a boy begins to find looking at a girl gives him a feeling of pleasure and a girl finds it enjoyable to look at a boy. This is called the age of puberty.

But here, also, girls and boys of that age are not able to mix together freely because they are still children. It is still like having a toy. So they have this feeling of pleasure but they do not yet know the purpose of it. So that, actually, if parents are not careful at that point, and they just let boys and girls mix together freely, there is the danger that they do not know the character of the children because some children have a good character and are well brought up and others are not and have bad habits. So by just mixing together freely they'll experiment until finally they find out how it works. So that is why at that age girls and boys should not be allowed to mix freely.

The human forces which permit children to really learn seriously, to study, come after puberty. It is only at that point that Bapak allows children to enter Subud and do the latihan. Starting today young people who want to be, may be opened at age seventeen. That is low enough because if they are younger than that they will not feel it as something important for their lives, but they will treat it as a pleasure and will not want to study any more. ...

Bapak concluded by saying:

It is God's will that we should worship Almighty God with our jiwas in the latihan kejiwaan and also use our heart and mind and our nafsu and our whole physical makeup to earn our living and to work in the world so that the jiwa and body develop together. And it is that parallel development which will enable us when we come to the moment of our death to leave behind the heart and mind and body and return fully conscious to the world from which we came. [Recording 83 LON 18]

After the Congress I went to stay with Marc Vouga in Lausanne, Switzerland, for a holiday. Marc was a successful architect with his own practice whom I had met through the Subud architects' group. I loved the beauty of the scenery and buildings, and the elegance of living. I visited other Subud families and joined in latihans and testing with members who had not been to the World Congress.

...

Back in Australia I wanted to resign from the Project Sunrise board, but again testing showed that the outcome of the project could, even then, yield a good result. As it went on, members of Subud from all over the world—architects, planners, economists and other professionals—offered their services (usually travelling at their own expense to Sydney to do so). They came and went, their advice largely ignored. Finally on 17 February 1984, convinced that the project had no hope of success, I sent my resignation to Bapak. He accepted it, but I felt that he was disappointed.

By the time the design report by Project Sunrise came out, it had influenced the New South Wales government to develop Darling Harbour, but Subud got nothing. Project Sunrise had accrued huge debts and many Subud members had lost their money.

Bapak described us as pioneers. Someone said, 'Pioneers often perish on the frontier'. As for the International Subud Centre, I believe we failed because we didn't use our latihan as guidance.

When I talk like this about Subud projects, my friends ask, 'Why do you have to make excuses? Couldn't Bapak have made a mistake in the people that he appointed?' Although Bapak never claimed to be exempt from error, for my part I will not criticise his judgement, as I believe he saw a bigger picture. But as for Bapak's responsibility, he did say at the outset that this project was not under Bapak's direction—it was a test, he said, for us to see if we could succeed on our own. Obviously, not yet!

~

Bapak looking at Project Sunrise's plans for Darling Harbour, Sydney. Left Luqman Keele and right Sharif Horthy translating, 1983

Delegates, members and children at Bapak's talk to the youth of Subud 14 August 1983 at the Anugraha Conference Centre, Windsor, England

Chapter Eleven

National Committee

In the turmoil of my last months with Project Sunrise salaries were not paid in full and sometimes not paid at all. The result was that I had completely used up my savings. I applied for, and got, the newly-created position of Executive Officer of the Civil and Mining Engineering Foundation at the University of Sydney. This was a half-time job requiring me to establish a liaison between the university and the engineering industry in New South Wales. It provided a basic income with time to rebuild my publishing business. I had come from Melbourne so it was also an opportunity to gain entry to the engineering profession in Sydney by meeting the academics, the heads of government utilities, and the chief executives of major engineering companies. I was given an office and, like the University staff, the freedom to arrange my own work program.

At this point I had a clear receiving that I should move into a larger apartment which had become available on the fourteenth floor of The Berkeley, in the CBD. Such accommodation in a new building seemed beyond my means but with that glow of feeling that accompanies the following of true guidance I went ahead, negotiating a lease and moved in. It had two bedrooms, one I used as a reception area, and a large sitting room which, with its wide view over Darling Harbour and the Pyrmont peninsula, made an ideal office. I began writing and designing engineering publications, first for the Foundation as part of my need for promotional literature. Then, by good fortune, the engineer who had been my principal client for publicity material in Melbourne took a position as a director of BHP Engineering and was transfered to Sydney.

Finding himself faced with the need to improve the technical literature for marketing he contacted me and offered me the production of a series of publications. I employed an illustrator and, as further work came in, Sandra Week joined me as secretary. Gradually work came in from other clients and for a time I employed a journalist to write project descriptions from my research. All were Subud members. Later David Week, who had an architectural business in Papua New Guinea, shared the office while he became established in Australia.

Meantime I continued to be active as a helper in the Sydney group. Then in March 1985 I had a dream in which Bapak's son Haryono indicated to me that I should be willing to work on the committee side of Subud. As this was a dream, I took it that I was meant to take the job for my personal experience, as much as for any help that I could give to Subud. (Perhaps all Subud activities can be seen in this light. Helpers are needed in Subud but also what they do is often largely of benefit to their own process.) The next month I attended the National Congress in Melbourne and was nominated chairman of the National Committee. I accepted and was elected.

The Subud organisation which had grown up under Bapak's guidance was clearly divided into spiritual and committee responsibilities. On the committee side it is a representative democracy. Members decide local policy and elect a committee to manage their affairs. Countries decide their national policy and elect a national committee. A committee councillor represents the country at a Subud World Congress held every four years. Policy is decided at the World Congress and is administered by the International Subud Committee (ISC) elected by Congress. In this way every member can contribute and participate. The spiritual side of Subud has a parallel structure of helpers at local, national and international level, appointed by Bapak.

Back in Sydney, Aisjah Parker agreed to be national secretary, bringing the professional skill of her many years as private secretary to the managing director of the large department store, David Jones, and her valuable experience on a previous National Committee.

I asked Helena Jansse to be the vice-chairwoman, both for her capability and as a deliberate move to include Subud's young people in a real, rather than a token, way. A previous local treasurer Raphael Favre, offered to be treasurer and the existing Committee Councillor Freeman Wyllie agreed to continue in office. With this strong team we set about doing our best to serve the needs of the membership across Australia. In the pleasant surroundings of the new office it was easy to enjoy ourselves, starting our Saturday meetings with festive breakfasts overlooking the harbour.

This harmony was to prove to be the basis of our capacity to achieve a great deal together during our two-year term.

Our task was to implement the policies of Congress and to act as an information service to the groups. Past National Committees had been largely autonomous in their work, refering back to group chairmen and women only on an adhoc basis. To overcome this disconnection a National Council was under consideration for the next Congress. Meanwhile we planned to foster the widest possible contact with the membership. Soon we found ourselves with long agenda and the need for fortnightly meetings. In June we took over the *Subud Australia Newsletter*. To speed up policy decisions we arranged for the groups to have telephones with speakers, and on Bapak's birthday held the first Australia-wide tele-conference, a ten-phone hookup. By getting local committees to gather around each speaker-phone, we were able to engage nation-wide participation.

With my strong bias towards helpers' work, it was natural that I should continue to be a champion of National Helpers' travel and latihan facilities, making sure that these were given priority within a balanced budget. This was a change in policy from the trend which had been leaving local services short of funds in order to meet high contributions to ISC.

Subud property ownership had been an important issue for many years in Australia, with several groups purchasing their own premises. Now congress had resolved to transfer all Subud halls into National ownership. This would make it easier for the properties to be used as a collective asset for buying new halls for other groups.

It was also a conscious move on my part to protect the existing latihan halls from being used by committees as collateral in enterprises at a time when there was great pressure locally and around the world to do this. (Members in several countries had mortgaged their houses to lend money to Anugraha.) The Sydney members probably still have their hall today because of this national ownership policy. When this transfer of ownership was completed Subud Australia (Inc) held the titles to the halls in Perth, Adelaide, Melbourne and Sydney. Subud Darwin meanwhile found a church hall for sale and asked for help to buy it. Although the group was only ten members, Subud Australia (Inc) agreed and I travelled to Darwin to negotiate the purchase, taking out a local bank mortgage.

The major task of the committee arising from the Congress resolutions was the incorporation of Subud Australia using Subud Human Welfare Incorporated (SHW Inc), a company limited by guarantee. In the process a new constitution for Subud Australia had to be prepared to bring it into line with that of Subud UK, the accepted International standard at the time. As the ten centres were to become the members of the new Subud Australia (Inc) it was also necessary to prepare a new Memorandum and Articles of Association and Regulations for the Subud centres, and register each under the Associations Incorporation Acts in each state. Throughout the first year in office I worked on these constitutions, falling back on Rod McKechnie (an accountant) for support. This turned out to be an enormous task, as each of the seven States had its own Act. The centre constitutions also had to be consistent and compatible with the new constitution of Subud Australia (Inc). The problem I had set myself was to achieve a common constitution for all centres which would meet all the legal requirements and be agreed to by the whole membership.

We took the draft to the National Congress held at Noalimba in Perth at Easter 1985. Those who were there will remember the patience needed to deal with constitutional matters from the rostrum. But we had done our homework and the Memorandum and Articles of Association and Regulations for the Constitution of Subud Australia and for the ten Subud Centres were adopted.

National Committee at the Australian Congress Perth 1985

Delegates play music and dance at Australian National Congress 1985

On return to Sydney we used a city law firm to handle the Subud Australia company registration. They went through the fine points required by Corporate Affairs and finally got permission to change the constitution and name of SHW Inc to Subud Australia (Inc).

During this time we worked with the National Dewan to arrange a four-day helpers' gathering at The University of Sydney St John's College. Groups of men and women from around Australia and New Zealand met and discussed topics of common interest which they then tested in smaller separate groups. It went well and was repeated later with members and helpers.

In the last weeks of my tenure I made a personal attempt to get the Australian International Centre project going again with a new initiative. I enlisted the help of David Week as architect to prepare a new proposal based on a largely residential component and presented this through the newsletter to the membership. However, the project had run out of steam and, although I had obtained Bapak's support, it never got beyond one committee meeting.

My two-year term as National Committee Chairman came to its end at the National Congress held in Sydney at Easter 1987. The committee had established a National Council and it had achieved three long-term goals: an international constitution for Subud Australia, incorporation of Subud nationwide, and the collective ownership of all latihan halls.

...

At dawn on the 23 June 1987, the morning following his birthday, Bapak died at his home in Pamulang, South Jakarta. When I heard, the latihan coursed through every atom of my being so that I stood, infused with inner life, entirely loving of Bapak. Then into this stillness, mute with respect, came the words: *The message is more important than the man.*

For three days I was in a crisis state as the latihan filled the infinite inner space left by Bapak's passing. With this latihan came a new strength like an inheritance—an inheritance with a clear responsibility.

Meantime towards the end of my term as National Chairman, I had started to receive inner questions about the meaning of my name. This was strange but insistent. I felt that it was a response to the tensions of that time. It persisted and on 16 October 1987 I asked a helper to test.

The questions and answers were like this:

'What is the meaning of Lamaan?'

(a voice) 'Faithful to God.'

The voice continued: 'His name should be Raymond, which means strength of the sun and equals masculine consciousness. … It also means not easily taken advantage of.'

I was surprised, but soon understood the significance of the test. My growing concern about my name had been an indication of a need for a change of attitude. I had, in those months of work on the Subud constitutions, allowed myself to be taken advantage of and my inner self was now indicating that I should not allow this to continue. Questioning my name was the way that my inner feeling prompted me to call up a different response in myself. Changing my name would be a confirmation of my commitment to this new response. It was time to be stronger and the name that symbolised this was Raymond. I knew that I needed to change my attitude and should change my name.

At first it was difficult to adopt the new name—it made a particular demand to bring something new into being. Gradually I began to see that it supported a change which I needed to make in other aspects of my Subud life. Although I had considered my activities in Subud as my conscious choice—as a helper, as a member of IDC assisting Bapak in Cilandak, or as National Chairman—I now realised that there was an unconscious aspect to my 'dedication'. For example, as a helper I had never turned away anyone who asked, although there were some who called at all hours for months before they came to stand on their own feet. Now I asked: Wasn't this the attitude Bapak had tested years earlier in Wellington: *How does a racehorse feel when being ridden in a race*?

I continued to be an active helper. Sydney had had a strong and numerous men helper's group for the years leading up to the 1989 Subud World Congress, but after Congress numbers had dwindled, with several helpers going overseas and interstate. Although we were few, members continued to come for testing and we had many valuable experiences. It would be out of place to discuss other people's testing, but I can relate one or two of my own receivings.

During this time we had a member from another group come to the general latihan. When it began I started to make a sound like an Aboriginal didjeridoo and in the same experience I felt suffocated by what I recognised were forces of Aboriginal culture. This was a totally new experience for me. I felt that the blowing out which made the sacred sound was connected with my need to surrender (let out) the pressure of the Aboriginal forces oppressing me. The experience was very interesting but I also realised that it was meaningful and was somehow connected with the visitor.

After the latihan he came to us and asked if the helpers could test something for him. We gathered two or three others and listened while he told us that he was finding his work very heavy and unsatisfactory. He said he was teaching adult Aboriginals. He had started out liking the job and entered into the task with enthusiasm. From what he said, I realised that he had been rating himself beneath his pupils. In his idealism, which was to respect the culture of the Aboriginal people, he had surrendered himself. I also understood, from the experience that I had just had in the latihan, that his pupils had a collective racial psyche (their spiritual cultural force) and that he, by losing himself in the face of that force, became overwhelmed by it. I knew also from my experience that, in the face of this Aboriginal force, it was necessary that he maintain his self-respect. In Subud terms he had to *inwardly separate* from the effect of his pupils' feelings and so avoid their nature from invading his inner feeling*. This understanding, which all came in a few minutes of latihan, was readily accepted by the visitor. It remained only for us to test with him so that he could experience the truth directly for himself.

* In Bapak's words: '... the inner feeling will awaken and be able to recognise the existence of the various kinds of life forces which flow in and out and move it.' (1969)

Some time later one of the members was diagnosed as having cancer and asked the helpers to do latihan with him. He was a particular friend and I was glad to take part. In the last weeks of May, as the illness progressed, although he had pain he showed great fortitude and remained cheerful. During one of the last latihans at his bedside I cried freely with deep sobbing. It was a latihan experience from beyond my heart and without sentiment or sadness. After half an hour it ended spontaneously, just it had started. My friend, who had not wept, said that he felt quite surrendered about dying as he was sure it was God's will. 'The only problem I have had,' he said, 'is that I have not been able to cry, perhaps because of my childhood in a Japanese concentration camp. Thank you, I needed to bawl, but could not. I feel relieved by your crying.'

...

In February 1992, coming home from an overseas trip to a disharmonious situation in the helpers' group in Sydney, rather than once again being drawn into the problem as requested I decided to become inactive as a helper. This was a major decision as I had been a helper continuously for more than thirty years. It was, however, the natural response of my new attitude and with it came a sense of relief and independence.

The decision was followed by an important dream:

I had been at the altar of a large cathedral and was coming out the side door. Instead of leaving the porch and going to the street, I turned back to enter the nave where the congregation sits. The porch was partitioned from the nave, and as I looked in my eyes were drawn up to the cathedral ceiling high above. I was filled with awe to see that it was a wondrous mandala pattern formed by the beams and vaults rising from a perfectly symmetrical square surround. Lowering my gaze I saw, showing above the partition, a crown on the head of a statue of a huge serpent. I assumed that it was part of a great sculpture of St George and the dragon in the midst of the nave, but I didn't see St George. Because of the partition I could only see the crowned dragon's head. It was exactly under the centre of the mandala ceiling.

The dream confirmed the rightness of my decision to withdraw from being an active helper. It showed that my decision was based on an important change in attitude from approaching the latihan as a helper (a priest at the altar) to approaching the latihan as a member (represented by the congregation). The importance of this change to my personal development was shown by the archetypal symbols: the mandala ceiling with its sense of wonder—a symbol of wholeness—and the crowned dragon* representing the transformation process.

What followed was an intensification of my latihan. I was beset with a burning need to find a higher source of moral guidance, to know *from a higher level* right from wrong and have the inner certainty to act accordingly. As my present value system lost its authority, I searched deeply in myself for an answer. It was all in vain; I was left in limbo. Gradually over several months a new viewpoint established itself. The problem had required a change of attitude—a spiritual change. Meanwhile the decision to withdraw from group activity released new energy for outer work.

~

* The crowned dragon was a strange image to occur in a Christian cathedral, but according to CG Jung it has the same meaning as the phoenix, a symbol applied to Christ's resurrection.

Chapter Twelve

Personal Enterprises

Whereas I had spent much of my working time in the last few months on Subud administration, I now felt some urgency to return to my own business*. Simply, I was approaching sixty and needed to provide for my retirement. I returned to writing and graphic art, travelling interstate to visit engineering and environmental projects. Gradually by my employing artists, photographers and printers, a small publishing enterprise emerged. When Ramzi Winkler decided to retire from PT IDC in Indonesia, I sponsored his move to Australia and registered a branch in WA.

BHP Engineering was the consulting arm of Australia's largest company so through them our publications came to the notice of other engineering consultants. Our main product was promotional literature—annual reports and brochures—but we also prepared exhibitions for trade fairs in Australia and mainland China. We continued the established glossy quarterly colour magazine for BHP Engineering, which was to run to a quarter of a million copies over eight years. For a time we shared offices with David Week. Drawing on his skill with the Macintosh computer we extended our work to BHP Steel and were awarded the contract to produce a series of illustrated operational and maintenance manuals for Australia's major steel plant. As this work required a staff of five we leased a larger office with a wide view of the Harbour. I employed Subud members and for a year the business prospered, providing us all with good incomes and making a profit for the company. Sandra Week continued working with me as secretary.

* Consulting Associates International Pty Ltd

All our staff were Subud members and I'm sure that their reliability and goodwill was a major factor in our prosperity at that time. (This good fortune extended to the BHP representative, who won a lottery and was able to retire at the end of the project.)

In August 1989 at the Subud World Congress in Sydney, I met Karsten Smith, a graphic artist from Vancouver. I showed him the work we were doing and suggested that we collaborate. When the next major brochure for BHP Engineering came around I travelled to Canada and worked with Karsten producing the concept design. From that time on I directed all my graphic artwork to him, making two further trips to his office in Vancouver. Karsten had a very fine art sense and his designs were appreciated by my clients.

In addition to the publicity business, I revived my engineering activity, applying computer analysis to the structural design of buildings in cyclone and earthquake zones of the Pacific—schools, a hospital, a cathedral, housing and new building methods for Aboriginal housing. I produced David Week's illustrated architectural book *Building Hotels in Papua New Guinea—A Cultural Approach*, sponsored by the European Community Development Fund. The same year I became associate editor of the magazine *Australian Concrete Construction*. Working as a journalist I interviewed people and wrote articles about current building projects in Victoria and New South Wales. Travelling again, I brought myself up-to-date with engineering development in Melbourne and Sydney.

In 1993 I turned to fulltime writing and co-authored the book *The Man From The East* * with Istimah Week. It was the story of her experiences near Bapak. It was an opportunity to participate in writing about life in Cilandak at the time I was there and about the latihan. I also researched the historical background. I did my best to keep my contribution secondary and supportive of Istimah's story, and to respect the spontaneity of her feelings.

I have not included many extracts from Bapak's Talks in this memoir as I felt that Bapak's explanations about Subud had been adequately covered in *The Man From The East.*

* Published by Vantage Press, New York 1996

Istimah Week's autobiographical account of Subud

The impetus for Istimah to write came, as she says in her Introduction, through the encouragement of her friends, as a record of her experiences with Bapak and as a token of her gratitude for the latihan. Unwavering support for her writing came from her husband Mark. For my part, I *had* to do it—my inner feeling had decided.

Then there was my sister, Tess, who became the editor. Strangely, her participation seems to have been presaged twenty years earlier.

On 28 June 1975 Tess wrote to me in Jakarta from Sydney. She said that her step-daughter Blanche d'Alpuget had been granted a Commonwealth scholarship to write a history of Subud. Would I do whatever I could to help with her request for permission from Bapak? Tess commended Blanche for the task, saying that she had lived for several years in Indonesia and that her recently-completed novel, although not published, had received acclaim from the Australian Fellowship of Writers. I came to learn later that Tess, who was journalist, had been Blanche's editor and adviser. Bapak declined permission and it was left to me to explain to Tess that the reason was that Blanche had no direct experience of the latihan on which to base her writing. So it was that a book about Subud by Blanche, with Tess as editor, did not proceed. Blanche went on to become one of Australia's best-known authors, writing several novels, including *Turtle Beach,* which was made into a film, and the biography of Bob Hawke, the Prime Minister, whom she later married. Blanche eventually was opened and became a regular member of Subud in Sydney.

When it came to working on Istimah's book, I approached Tess for advice. I asked her because I knew of her experience as an author including, appropriately, the book *The Religions of Australia**. I later discovered that she was also an editor and had been Executive Editor of Books at *The Reader's Digest.* I had completely forgotten the episode with Blanche. Tess agreed to become the editor of Istimah's book.

* Published by Rigby in 1970.

Tess van Sommers (Mrs Lou d'Alpuget) author, journalist and book editor

As I worked on the manuscript of *The Man From The East* I was not only making a transition from technical to biographical writing but also I was moving unsuspectingly out of full-time work. By mid-1994 I had withdrawn from my engineering and publishing contracts and my inner feeling, which seemed to be making the decisions, left me little option but to formally retire. I was happy to go along with this and began by tidying up my personal archives.

The first thing was to type my mother's story of her life with my father, which had come to light among family papers. From this I was drawn to know more about the places where we had lived in my earliest years. In June 1994 I hired a campervan and travelled over the route of my parents' wagon journey (1931-1934) through Victoria and New South Wales, following my mother's written account.

I was deeply affected, as can be gauged by this letter which I wrote to my sister Tess, who had been on this journey as a young girl:

> My trip along the route of our family's four-year wagon journey made during the Great Depression was a very important and healing experience. I started out with no recollections of that time (I was only three years old when it started) but I followed my mother's joys and sufferings by reading her story while I was surrounded by the places and conditions that she encountered. I consciously put my normal judging self aside and let the impressions enter me like a child. The result was that a part of me that was unconscious emerged. I can't say how much this connected with the feelings of the small boy who originally made the journey.
>
> Where I had no recollection of anything visible, I began to realise that I had been carrying obscure feelings of that unknown childhood, feelings that, for some reason, I had never acknowledged. The effect of this unconscious part of me emerging was that a burden was dispelled. It was like a mist lifted and the feeling revealed beneath was easy, simple, accepting—the emotional state of a child. In this condition I stopped thinking and criticising, and yet, unlike a child, I still had my adult awareness.

Not only was this a fulfilling experience which has added to my wholeness, and changed me, but also it has resulted in my being left with a new connection with our father, my mother and with you, my older sister Tess. Whether this connection is a product of the journey or is related to the original unconscious knowledge, I don't know. But as Jung would say, 'The experience itself was real for me.' In some way I have redeemed my parents. The burden I carried before the journey may well have been their troubles. If it was their sins, they are now—in my psyche anyway—forgiven. I now feel only love for them.

I can't leave this account without acknowledging the latihan. Throughout the journey, the latihan was never far away, often filling me with gratitude to God. As I sped along a country road, these feelings came out as a spontaneous cry into the wind and the vast spaces around ... 'Allahu Akbar. Allahu Akbar.'

Retracing the wagon journey raised many questions about the early years of my father's life and his work. To answer these I got his military record from the Australian Archives and found where he was buried. I traced a few examples of his work as an artist before the war which showed that he was a talented and experienced painter. I was able to investigate his post-war career as a writer and poet by going through the newspapers and magazines of the period. For the rest there were notes by the family which gave the flavour of his life: 'brimming with whimsical humour ... well-read and versed in all the arts.' In this desire to know my father I felt the latihan cleansing some essential connection. I wept at his grave.

By the end of 1995 *The Man From The East* was complete and I had arranged for it to be published the following July in New York. It was my hope that it would reach a wide public readership. When it was clear that the publisher was having little success in selling through his agencies, I concentrated on distribution through SPI, UK, Subud USA, and other Subud outlets. As it sold, Istimah received many letters of appreciation, including one from the director of the Vatican Library, Leonard Boyle, who found it 'fascinating and uplifting'. The book enjoyed its best sales to the public during the 1997 Subud World Congress in Spokane, USA.

During the last days of the Congress men and women met separately to test 'how to bring the latihan into daily life'. This question arose from Istimah Week's description of 'inner separation' in *The Man From The East.* Forty women attended the testing with Istimah.

In the smaller men's group after doing latihan together, each one tested two questions to do with a recent incident in their lives where they were overwhelmed by an emotional reaction:

First (to re-experience the reaction): What did I feel when I reacted?

Then immediately afterwards: What is the feeling of being inwardly separated from this reaction and its cause?

Each person reported experiencing a state of separation of their inner feeling from the emotion—a state which the latihan could bring into their daily life. This separation is described by Bapak in many talks. This is from the 1969 *Basis and Aim of Subud* booklet:

... in the latihan kejiwaan of Subud one really feels that one's inner self is no longer influenced by the passions, heart and mind, which means that in the latihan kejiwaan of Subud the inner feeling has truly been separated from their influence.

Why should the passions, heart and mind be separated from the inner feeling, when these are man's most important equipment for his life in this world, which can be used to increase and broaden his knowledge? It is because, unless the passions, heart and mind are separated from the inner feeling, it will not be able to be in a pure state in receiving the latihan kejiwaan, so that it will be impossible for the inner feeling to receive the contact from the Great Life Force which in fact has permeated it inwardly and outwardly.

Letters after the Congress confirmed the value of this experience and the recognition that this separation is known to everyone who does the latihan, but is not always put into practice in daily life.

After the 1997 World Congress, Istimah accepted an offer from Amalia Sanchez Caballero in Argentina to translate her book into Spanish. I took on the role of publisher, travelling to Chile, Istimah's country, to arrange the editing, and then printing it in Australia as *El Hombre del Este*. It was well received, particularly in in Spain, Colombia and Cuba.

The Congress also opened up new opportunities for me to write about the Subud experiences of others. It started with an offer by a Subud sponsor and the ISC media group to prepare a collection of Bapak's explanations which were not in his talks and his correspondence. This was to include members' accounts of meetings with Bapak. Jerry Chalem, whose team was making video-tape interviews at the Congress, offered to provide transcripts for the project. Back in Australia I began research in Harlinah Longcroft's *History of Subud* archives and had completed about 100 selections from Subud magazines when the sponsor had to withdraw. The association with Harlinah led to assisting her with the preparation of the illustrations for the *History of Subud, Volume 1, Book 2*, which describes the eventful coming of Subud to Coombe Springs in 1957. This was followed by writing the story of the first ten years of *PT International Design Consultants 1966-1976* for a later volume (reproduced in part in the Appendix).

Here I draw this memoir to a close with a short epilogue, and the hope that those who have followed my experiences through these pages have been able to take away something of value to themselves and of benefit to others about life in Subud.

All Praise be to God.

Epilogue 2003

As with others of my generation, ageing has brought new responsibilities and interests into my life in Subud. Where my helper activity in the past was directed exclusively to my brothers and sisters in Subud, it is now shared with the needs of others, and with more time devoted to my affection for relations and friends who do not yet have the latihan.

The way of sharing the benefit of the latihan with those not yet in Subud is the same as 'helping'—quiet attentiveness—but adapted to each situation by the inner feeling. This does not mean imposing anything on another person or intruding in any way into their privacy. It is just the responsibility that receiving the latihan carries, to manage one's own actions and reactions in a constructive way—known in Subud as *Susila*, right living.

As I see it now, everyone I meet is a participant in my life and, to the extent that the guidance of the latihan suggests it, they become part of my life in Subud.

Meanwhile, within the brotherhood of Subud members continue to be served by the active helpers who carry on Bapak's mission. For them Bapak has left in his many talks signposts like this:

If people always love you and respect you and always ask you for advice, for help, then that is the proof that there is within you the nature of the Insan Kamil, *that is, the perfect man. ... And (with the latihan) this will progress to higher and higher levels.*

[Recording 82 SYD1]

~

Appendix

Reference

*PT International Design Consultants**

Bapak founded International Design Consultants (IDC) in November 1966 when he called Ramzi Winkler, Abdullah Pope and Lamaan van Sommers to set up a company of architects and engineers in Jakarta. All three had already helped Bapak with the early development of land in Cilandak, South Jakarta, purchased by Bapak in 1960 in order to build an International Subud Centre.

In October 1975, Bapak described IDC in this way in an address to the staff:

IDC is a company or enterprise which does not just seek to make profits, but is a company which seeks to make a living so that it can be said to maintain the life of society. … It is not an enterprise that seeks profits just for itself, or for its own group, but for the general good. Therefore it does not follow the way of capitalism. It teaches and trains you, the workers and staff, so that you can work properly, so that you can stand on your own feet. In so doing, this policy follows the will of Almighty God that people should divide the profits they obtain equally or fairly, so that life on earth can be safe and happy.

It is very necessary that people should really go in for activities which have the quality of development. Development does not just mean building houses, but developing everything which is in the inner self. They should become skilled or clever, and capable, and have a firm character, so that they can believe in themselves and not always have to be dependent on someone else for their living.

* Written for the *History of Subud,* Vol 3, Book 2—The Latihan and Commerce: PT International Design Consultants, The First Ten Years—1966 to 1976 Edited 21 June 2000. (Part only reproduced here.)

Therefore, as Bapak explained long ago, you should not just work as labourers. No! Work as if it is for the sake of your own interests and for your own needs. In the same spirit the directors for their part should not feel that they have authority so that they only consider themselves to be important. No, they must give importance to the whole enterprise, not just to themselves.

If this kind of thing can be done by you and by our people of Indonesia, as well as by the people of other countries, the world will become orderly, just and prosperous. [Recording 75 CDK 8]

The three partners called by Bapak in 1966 had joined Subud at Coombe Springs in 1957 and had in the intervening years each found his way to Indonesia.

Lamaan van Sommers was an Australian structural engineer who had supervised the construction of the Gurdjieff meeting hall at Coombe Springs. In September 1959, during Bapak's second visit to England, Bapak invited him to Indonesia. In May 1960 he travelled to Jakarta, arriving just before the Cilandak land was purchased. Bapak asked him to design a two-storey guesthouse with nine bedrooms and dining facilities, which he did, staying six months and seeing the building construction started.

Abdullah Pope was an English architect who had in January 1962 first visited Indonesia on his way home to the UK from working in the USA. He stayed a year and worked for the Jakarta City Council. In January 1965 he returned again to Jakarta and worked for six months as an architectural supervisor on the new Australian Embassy building. During this time he helped with the design of a house for Bapak. He then had to leave because of the political unrest.

Ramzi Winkler was a German architect who had arrived in Indonesia in December 1962, having asked Bapak if he could help with Cilandak. He designed Bapak's house and supervised its construction for three years until it was finished in April 1966. During this time on Bapak's advice he took a position as an architect for the new German Chancery building and lived in Jakarta through the September 1965 coup d'etat disturbances.

Each of the three partners was a qualified professional and each brought several years of experience in building design and construction to the enterprise. Abdullah had specialised in office design, Ramzi in construction supervision, and Lamaan in structural design and project management. Their years of working in large companies and in various countries had prepared them to be self-reliant in a developing environment. The timing was good. Indonesia was beginning to open again to the outside world after two decades of political and economic isolation.

When Bapak suggested that Abdullah, Ramzi and Lamaan start a company together, he said that they should look for work in Indonesia—outside Subud. It was to be a business based on architectural and engineering skills which could be called on to help when necessary with the development of Cilandak.

A company registered under the Foreign Investment Law offered the best means for the expatriate partners to be allowed to stay in Indonesia and establish a business. This law had been set up to encourage overseas companies to invest in Indonesian ventures, many of which would require architects and engineers. When a joint venture was proposed a year later, Bapak suggested that Ir Haryono, a chemical engineer, and Wahana, a lawyer, should be the local counterparts.* Bapak agreed to be Chairman of the Board.

The company was named PT International Design Consultants.†

* In September 1967 Abdullah, Ramzi and Lamaan prepared a letter of intent to the Minister of Public Works (PUT) applying for permission to set up a company under the Foreign Investment Law, which had been promulgated earlier that year. In December they were referred for advice to Ir Soehoed, Vice-Chairman of the Indonesian Foreign Investment Board, an engineer with his own consultancy. He was very supportive of the three bringing their professional skills to his country and suggested that they apply for permission to establish a 100 percent foreign owned company, with provision to make 30 percent of the shares available to Indonesian nationals after five years. Although they could only hope to raise US$10,000 in capital, he said that he would recommend the submission. (Footnotes continued on the next page.)

Although in 1966 Bapak did not refer to IDC as a *Subud Enterprise*, it was one of a line of enterprises of Subud members that he had earlier fostered with local members in Indonesia—trading businesses, a bank and a contracting company. IDC was the first with expatriates. The aim of the three partners was to carry out all aspects of their work together according to the principle of Subud—*right living concordant with the Will of God.* Years later Bapak was to speak of this principle being attained through *Enterprise* and would describe IDC as an example of a *Subud Enterprise.*

The three partners set up an office in the original latihan building in Cilandak, next to Bapak's Secretariat. Their first project was the renovation of the Australian Ambassador's Residence in Menteng. This modest beginning led to more work—a shoe polish factory for PT Kiwi, an Australian investor. Factory projects were to become a mainstream activity and were to increase in size and complexity to include several of the major pharmaceutical factories built in Jakarta in the next ten years—Ciba Geigy for the Swiss, Natterman for the Germans, Warner Lambert for the Americans, and many others. The partners found that initially work came to them almost without asking. The harder they worked, the more projects were offered to them.

* *(Continued)* In January 1969 the submission was revised to be a joint-venture company with 30 per cent Indonesian shareholdings. The partners offered the whole 30 per cent to Bapak, but he declined and instead suggested Haryono and Wahana represent the local counterpart. In February 1969, PUT forwarded the application to the Foreign Investment Board and in February, after changes defining the company's work as 'Human Skill Investment', the Board approved the application. The Foreign Investment Board Sub-Committee approved the application. No more was heard of the submission until May 1970 when Erling Week was managing IDC and he hired Dr Santoso of the international accountants Arthur Young to re-apply. IDC received the President's signature on 27 June 1970. The Minister of PUT issued the 'Permit to Work' on 11 September 1970, and Haryono and Wahana registered PT IDC as a limited liability company on 25 September 1970.

It was largely due to the support of Ir Soehoed that the expatriate partners were able to obtain visas and work in Indonesia during the three years it took for IDC to be granted permission to operate as a company.

† PT is an abbreviation for Persoalan Terbatas meaning Proprietary Limited.

The first task of the partners was how to expand the enterprise—engage new staff, provide office space and buy equipment. Recruiting was an unexpected problem. Bapak said that if there were no architects or engineers available from among the Indonesian Subud members then non-members could be employed, so long as the management was in Subud hands. However, in 1967, after decades of anti-colonial national sentiment, and almost twenty years of anti-Western rhetoric under President Sukarno, many Indonesians were reluctant to work with a foreign company. Nevertheless this gradually changed and in the years that followed eighty percent of new employees were recruited outside Subud.

An architectural and engineering consultancy is a complex business. It has to create buildings within hundreds of social, technological, environmental and economic constraints. Every project is unique. First the partners study in depth the client's needs —the processes of a factory, the functioning of a school, the uses of an office building, or the pattern of life of a whole township. This information, which may run to volumes, is developed into proposals and then into a design with engineering calculations, drawings, specifications, cost estimates, tender documents and construction timetables. After the contract is awarded the construction is supervised for quality and for cost compliance. For the documentation, senior architectural and engineering design staff are needed, supported by draftsmen, quantity surveyors, project managers and quality control supervisors. An administrative team takes care of finance, employment, office space and equipment. Everyone from manager to clerk is essential to the operation.

Another complexity is the extent of the information required. It includes building codes and practices; current material, labour and equipment costs; government regulations; company law, taxation and insurance conditions; and local knowledge about contractors and construction rates.

Bapak had at first said little about the direction of IDC's work. The partners had set up the company as a consultancy, a form which maintains independence from the building contractor.

The alternative is where the architects and engineers are also part of a construction company. Sometime in the early years Bapak said that he would like IDC to go beyond designing buildings and into construction. The three partners felt that they did not have enough local knowledge of labour employment, equipment hiring, financing, etc. and did not attempt it.

Bapak did not press the issue. It was to be six years after the founding of IDC before Bapak set up a company to construct the S.Widjojo office building in Jakarta. By then it was clear that Bapak's vision for a building company was total management—as a developer—included self-financing through a Subud bank.

IDC had started with assets of only US$2,000 but two years later the partners were able to buy a half-hectare parcel of land south of the Subud compound for an office and directors' housing. They put a simple timber building on the street front, giving IDC office working space and its own public entrance.

In 1967 Bapak suggested to Sharif Horthy that he come to Indonesia. Sharif had graduated in physics and civil engineering in UK, and had worked for a time as a structural engineer with Ove Arup, a leading international engineering consultancy. At first Sharif worked at investigating business opportunities in Indonesia with Erling Week, who had personally been invited to live in Wisma Subud by Bapak. In June 1969 Sharif joined IDC full time. In March 1970, Lambert Gibbs, an English architect who had also been at Coombe Springs in 1957, left his successful design practice in UK to come to Indonesia and join IDC.

In 1969, Irwan Maindonald, a New Zealand mechanical and electrical engineer, decided to set up an Indonesian branch of his building services consultancy to work with IDC. He called it Asian Area Consultants (AAC). This company became vital to IDC as the need grew to work closely with the engineers designing the electrical, water and air-conditioning services for pharmaceutical manufacturing plants and other sophisticated buildings.

In May 1970 Bapak, at Sharif's suggestion, asked Erling Week to act as Manager of IDC. Under his direction the Indonesian President's approval was obtained and IDC was able to be registered as a company under the Foreign Investment Law. This law carried with it the important provision of long-term visas for expatriate company directors.

IDC grew steadily into a significant consulting business in Jakarta. As the company expanded, financing became critical and the partners had to arrange loans for working capital. This was resolved by increasing the company's share capital from US$10,000 to US$100,000 and converting the outstanding loans to shares. Sharif and Irwan became directors. IDC was four years old and was enjoying the confidence of being under Bapak's guidance and the optimism that pervaded business life in Indonesia. Its list of factories was growing and it had added office buildings, schools, a sports club and several houses.

When Sharif and Lambert joined the team IDC had enough new contracts for them each to manage his own project. The directors came together only at weekly project meetings and at monthly Board meetings on company policy. As a result, for a time IDC became a group of independent project managers sharing the staff and facilities.

Meanwhile towards the end of 1970 Bapak began to prepare Cilandak to act as host to the Fourth Subud World Congress. No international conference facilities existed in Jakarta. Although IDC was occupied with the design of its largest pharmaceutical factories and the Joint Embassy School, and the partners were busy with the construction of their own houses, they took on the extensive preparations for the Congress. Sharif and Abdullah designed a new latihan hall. Ramzi designed and supervised construction of temporary accommodation built entirely of bamboo for 1000 people. Lamaan designed and installed new electricity generation plant and deep aquifer pumping equipment for water.

A year later Sharif transferred from PT IDC to head a construction company for Bapak, which later became PT S.Widjojo. When Ir Haryono returned from the UK in April 1973 the IDC Board decided to separate the administration from the project work of the technical directors and asked him to become Managing Director. Maksum Stafford, a retired Company Secretary from the UK living in Cilandak, joined him and they set about improving accounting and company reporting, regularising staff conditions, and introducing policies to include senior staff in the management.

In the next two years the number of employees rapidly increased from thirty to a peak of seventy-five as the company embarked on two major projects—a new township for INCO's large nickel mine on Sulawesi and the engineering for Bapak's special project, the S.Widjojo building. As IDC prospered the income was distributed to the employees as housing, transport and medical allowances, and bonuses.

In Bapak's talk to IDC on 31 October 1975 (page 231) he described the principles and attitudes to which the company aspired. The personal stories of the directors show that these ideals were arrived at gradually. They were not the result of a policy laid down by Bapak at the beginning or even by prompting later. They were the outcome of a natural growth towards human values as a result of the directors working together and following the latihan privately in their daily lives.

Bapak

Haryono

Sharif Horthy

Lamaan van Sommers

Abdullah Pope

Ramzi Winkler

Wahana

Irwan Maindonald

Bapak and the IDC directors at the IDC Idul Fitri celebration 1975

Nattermann pharmaceutical factory designed by Ramzi Winkler IDC

Nattermann factory at night from the Jakarta-Bogor highway

Ciba Geigy pharmaceutical factory designed by Lambert Gibbs, IDC

Ciba Geigy office and employees' canteen

Part of the 600 houses and community buildings of the INCO township

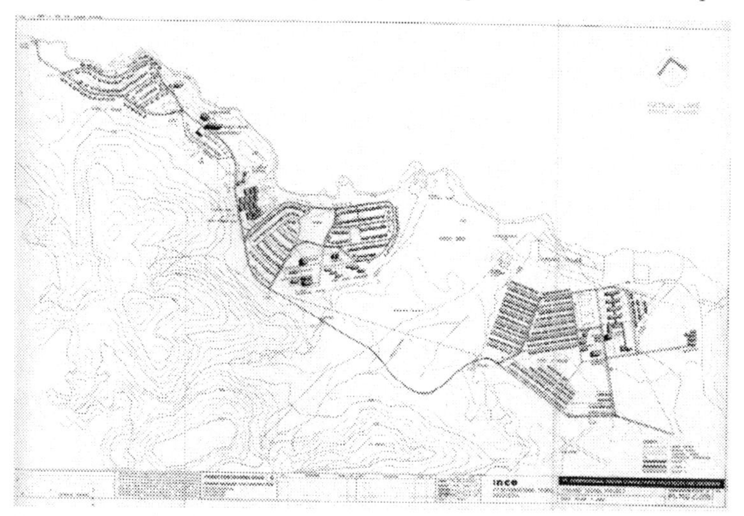

IDC Layout Plan for the west end of the INCO new township, Sulawesi

Glossary

Bapak	Indonesian word for Father—used for a respected older man. In this book it refers to Pak Subuh.
Pak Subuh	Bapak Muhammad Subuh Sumohadiwidjojo.
Subuh	Indonesian word meaning dawn. Also the Islamic dawn prayer, Subuh. Bapak was given the name Subuh because he was born at dawn. The word Subuh has no connection with the word Subud.
Ibu	Indonesian word for mother in Indonesian and a term of respect. In this book it refers to Bapak's wife Siti Sumari.
Cilandak	the suburb of South Jakarta where Pak Subuh established his home and the first International Subud Centre.
Contact	initial receiving of the latihan, also known as opening.
Helpers	those who according to Bapak have had enough experience of the latihan kejiwaan to be able to explain Subud and to pass on the contact to others.
Jiwa	spiritual content of the self, usually translated as soul.
Kejiwaan	Indonesian word meaning spiritual.
Latihan	Indonesian word which literally translates as training or exercise. Here it means the spiritual exercise of Subud.
Nafsu	the passions that animate feeling and thinking.
Testing	the name given to receiving answers to questions in the latihan state. Its function is to check the progress of the latihan or to gain insight into a problem.